Copyright Page

Stop Stepping on Rakes: Laugh at Your Mistakes, Learn from Them, and Keep Moving Forward

Copyright © January 01, 2025 by Ken Konet, M.Ed., MBA

All rights reserved. No part of this publication may be reproduced, distributed, or transmitted in any form or by any means, including photocopying, recording, or other electronic or mechanical methods, without the prior written permission of the publisher, except in the case of brief quotations used in critical reviews and certain other noncommercial uses permitted by copyright law.

For permission requests, write to the publisher at the address below:
Published by Humbolton Press
Dallas, Texas

www.Humbolton.com

This book is a work of nonfiction. The advice and strategies contained herein are based on the author's personal experience and research but should not replace professional guidance where appropriate. Any similarity to real persons, living or dead, is purely coincidental. (Unless it's you stepping on a rake—then yes, we're talking about you.)

Cover & Interior Design by: Ken Konet
First Edition: 2025
ISBN: 978-1-966703-01-3

Printed in the United States of America

Disclaimer

Disclaimer: *Read at Your Own Risk (and Laugh While You're at It)*

The content in *Stop Stepping on Rakes: Laugh at Your Mistakes, Learn from Them, and Keep Moving Forward* is provided for general informational and entertainment purposes only. It is not intended to be a substitute for professional advice, diagnosis, or treatment. If you're dealing with medical, psychological, financial, or other serious issues, please consult a qualified professional who knows what they're doing—because let's face it, this book is not a replacement for therapy, your doctor, or your accountant.

The author, publisher, and anyone remotely involved in the creation of this book disclaim all responsibility for any decisions, actions, or consequences resulting from its use. In short: if you take my advice and it goes sideways, don't sue me. Instead, laugh about it and learn from it.

Oh, and if you find a typo or two, let's call it "character." Nobody's perfect, not even authors.

About Me

About the Author: I'm a fellow human doing their best (**Spoiler:** I'm also a Work in Progress). I make mistakes every day, and now laugh about them.

Oh, hey there! You're holding my book, which either means you're stuck in life, bored out of your mind, or were guilt-tripped into buying this by someone who swears I changed their life. Either way, welcome! I'm Ken Konet—writer, instructional designer, IT engineer, and certified expert in turning life's messes into marginally less messy victories.

I've spent decades trying to figure out how to navigate this wild carnival called existence. Sometimes I've soared, and sometimes I've stepped on metaphorical (and literal) rakes. Trust me, it's all fun and games until your forehead becomes a hysterical roadmap for poor decisions. But here's the thing: I've learned that success isn't about being perfect, it's about falling flat on your face, laughing at your own ridiculousness, and stubbornly getting back up, anyway.

If my life were a resume (please don't steal this for LinkedIn), it would look like this:

- Two MBAs, a master's in education, and a PhD in How to Avoid Stepping on Rakes (self-taught).
- Years spent in IT engineering, dodging blue screens of death and figuring out why your Wi-Fi keeps cutting out (hint: it's always the router).
- A career as an instructional designer, which involves teaching people how to learn, unlearn, and hopefully remember to save their work before the power goes out.
- Countless hours of overthinking, procrastinating, and trying to outsmart my own ADHD brain.

When I'm not writing snarky how-to guides, you'll find me passionately enabling others—whether it's creating corporate training programs, helping people embrace failure as their greatest teacher, or teaching life lessons to anyone who accidentally makes eye contact with me at Starbucks.

I'm also a walking contradiction: A lover of motorcycles, camping, and hiking, who also cherishes quiet moments tinkering with technology or over-analyzing why we're all here (not in a deep philosophical way, just... why are we *here* in this meeting?).

This book isn't just another self-help manual. It's a battle cry for anyone who's tired of being stuck in the same loop of procrastination, doomscrolling, and telling themselves they'll "start tomorrow." (Spoiler: You won't.) I'm here to help you break the cycle, one awkward, imperfect, hilarious step at a time.

So, buckle up, buttercup. We're diving into chaos together. And remember: Progress isn't about the size of the step—it's about having the guts to take it in the first place (even if you're stepping on a rake).

Now, let's get unstuck and make some magic happen. Or at least avoid knocking ourselves out with another rake. Deal?

Why *Stop Stepping on Rakes*? Because I Lived It!

Let me tell you about the moment I discovered what it truly means to "step on a rake." Spoiler alert: it's not a metaphor. Nope, it's literal, painful, and life-altering. And it's exactly why I named this book *Stop Stepping on Rakes*. Consider it a tribute to the most embarrassing night of my life—a cautionary tale wrapped in teenage laziness and bad decision-making.

Picture this: 15-year-old me, the embodiment of peak teenage brilliance, standing in my parents' backyard at night. Why? Because earlier that day, my mom, a real estate agent who had a knack for attracting clients with kids who treated lawn tools like jungle gyms, kept telling me to clean up the yard. "Ken, put the tools away. Ken, turn off the shed light. Ken, stop being a lazy sack of hormones." You know, the usual mom stuff.

But did I listen? Of course not. I had important teenager things to do—like sitting. So, I procrastinated, thinking, *What's the worst that could happen?* (Spoiler: THIS. This is what happens.)

Eventually, after a Cleveland summer sunset in the glorious year of 1979, my guilt—or maybe my mom's voice echoing in my head—got the better of me, and I trudged outside to handle the tools in the pitch-black darkness, barefoot of course. Because why use daylight or wear shoes when you can risk your life instead?

Now, enter the rake. Not just any rake. This was a steel-tined dead grass pulling murder machine, lying in wait, perfectly positioned in the grass like a ninja assassin. My foot came down, and BAM—those tines pierced my bare skin and plunged into my foot like they were auditioning for a bloody slasher movie.

And WHACK! The handle snapped up and smacked me in the face. Full cartoon-style chaos. If I had an audience, they'd be rolling on the ground laughing while I let out a string of curse words that would've made a sailor blush. I, however, was bleeding, stunned, and having a very personal conversation with gravity.

I hobbled to the back door like a wounded animal, crawled up the steps, and dragged myself inside, leaving a bloody breadcrumb trail worthy of a true crime docuseries. My sister came home from a date, took one look at the large streak of blood on the floor, and went into full panic mode. But this was 1979—no cell phones, no instant reassurance. She had to sit there, staring at the mess, imagining the worst, until my parents brought me home from the Emergency Room.

At the hospital, the staff got an eyeful. "How did this happen?" they asked, with a mix of concern and barely concealed amusement. Let's just say explaining how you got into a fight with a rake and lost is no confidence booster, especially for a quirky teenage boy. One nurse couldn't hold back and quipped, "What's up, Doc? Been hanging out with Wile E. Coyote?" while another chimed in with, "Did the rake win, or is it just waiting for round two?" Their laughter echoed down the hallway as I sat there, red-faced, silently swearing vengeance against the entire gardening tool industry… wishing for a hole to crawl into.

When we got back home, my mom wasn't exactly brimming with sympathy. Yes, she got me patched me up, but her first words were...? "I told you to put the tools away earlier for a reason." That's mom code for "I hope this hurts enough that you'll never ignore me again and that you'll learn from this mistake."

My dad, of course, couldn't resist shaking his head and saying, "Guess the rake really *handled* you, huh?" before chuckling at his own genius. As he walked away, rounding the corner, he looked back at me, smirked, and said, "Well, at least you didn't *rake* in too much damage... oh, wait." I couldn't help but laugh, even through the pain—because honestly, it *was* funny, and I knew he meant well. And boy, did it hurt. Three holes in my foot and a comical cartoon-style knot on my forehead make a definite lifelong impression.

Here's the thing: that night wasn't just about physical pain. It was a life lesson delivered with the subtlety of a rake handle to the face. It's a story I've carried with me ever since—a reminder of how laziness, procrastination, and ignoring good advice can literally come back to hit you in the head and stab you in the foot.

So, why *Stop Stepping on Rakes*? Because that's what this book is all about: learning from the stupid stuff we all do, the painful lessons we'd rather forget, and the trails of metaphorical blood we leave behind while we figure life out. Hopefully, by the time you close this book, you'll have fewer rakes in your path—and you'll know how to avoid the ones that are still there.

And if nothing else, you'll think twice before walking barefoot in your backyard at night. Trust me on that one too.

How to Use This Book

Welcome to the part of the book where I convince you not to let this masterpiece collect dust under your coffee mug or, worse, end up as a makeshift paperweight. This isn't *just* another self-help book; it's a guide, a cheerleader, and, occasionally, a snarky drill sergeant here to help you stop stepping on life's rakes.

And yes, there will be rakes. Lots of rakes. But here's the good news: I packed every chapter with relatable Kenisms (like tiny nuggets of wisdom wrapped in sarcasm), pauses for reflection (because we all need a timeout), and even a TL;DR. Plus, there's homework. Don't groan—it's the fun kind that actually helps.

Let's break it down:

Step 1: Read It Your Way

No rules here, my friend. Start at the beginning, jump to the middle, or close your eyes and point to a random chapter. Life's unpredictable, so why should this book be any different? Think of it as a choose-your-own adventure for personal growth.

Step 2: Actually, Do Stuff

Sure, reading is great, but progress happens when you *do*. Each chapter has action steps, thought-provoking questions, and even homework (don't worry, no grades). Jot down notes, doodle in the margins, or type ideas into your phone's notes, just do something. Pro tip: Start with one small step. It takes time to overcome avoidance.

Step 3: Laugh, Roll Your Eyes, Repeat

The book features humor, sarcasm, and the occasional "ouch, that hit close to home" moment. If you laugh, cry, or find yourself muttering, "Why is this guy so relatable?" you're doing it right. Growth is uncomfortable, messy, and surprisingly funny when you look at it from the right angle.

Step 4: Take Breaks and Reflect

Some chapters might feel like a gentle nudge; others might feel like a rake to the face. That's intentional. At key moments, you'll find *Pauses for Reflection*—little pit stops to help you catch your breath, gather your thoughts, and consider how you'll dodge the next rake. Use these moments. They're here for you.

Step 5: Use the Extras

Every chapter ends with a recap, key takeaways, a Kenism to tie it all together, and a TL;DR summary for when you just need the bullet points. You'll also find cheat sheets and simple-to-follow homework that won't make you want to hurl this book across the room.

Step 6: Treat It Like Your Life Coach

This book isn't magic, and it won't solve your problems overnight. But if you treat it like a wise (and slightly sarcastic) friend, it'll guide you through the chaos. Revisit chapters when life throws you a curveball or when you're back on the rake-stepping train.

Step 7: Share the Love

If something in this book makes you go, "Wow, that actually worked," share it. Whether it's with a friend, coworker, or your social media followers, spreading good advice is like planting seeds of less-rakey lives.

Final Thoughts

This book is your map, guide, and partner-in-crime for navigating life's garden of opportunities (and rakes). So, dive in, take what resonates, and remember: every rake that whacks you in the face is just another lesson in disguise. Let's laugh, learn, and grow together—because life's too short to keep stepping on the same old rakes.

Now, go forth and conquer. Or at least avoid a few forehead smacks along the way. You've got this!

Stop Stepping on Rakes: Laugh at Your Mistakes, Learn from Them, and Keep Moving Forward

Table of Contents

Copyright Page 1
Disclaimer 2
About Me 3
Why *Stop Stepping on Rakes*? Because I Lived It! 5
How to Use This Book 8
Introduction: Welcome to the Garden 13
Chapter 1: Congratulations, You're a Hot Mess (But Fixable) 25
Chapter 2: Why Nothing Has Worked (Yet) 38
Chapter 3: Baby Steps for Grown-Ups 52
Chapter 4: How to Fail Like a Pro 66
Chapter 5: Stop Chasing Motivation—Build Momentum Instead 79
Chapter 6: When Life Hands You Lemons, Throw Them at a Wall .. 94
Chapter 7: Staying on Track (Even When You Want to Burn It All Down) 108
Chapter 8: The Setback Symphony—Embracing the Chaos 123
Chapter 9: How to Make the Momentum Last 137
Chapter 10: The Big Picture—Crafting a Life That Feels Like Your Own 151
Conclusion: The Last Chapter, but Just the Beginning 165
FAQs/FAFs: Frequently Asked Questions/Fails 177
Final Things to Think About 191

Notes:

Introduction: Welcome to the Garden

Kenism: *"Life, much like a garden, offers us a vast array of opportunities—some are ripe with possibility, others tangled with thorns. Every time we step forward, it is as though we step onto the soil of our experiences, planting seeds of action that will grow into the fruits of our future. But, too often, we step on a rake. We don't notice the obstacles until it's too late—until the handle springs up to smack us in the face. You see, the rake is not a punishment. It's a reminder. Today's attention determines the future. So, let's begin by stepping carefully, but let us not be afraid of the rake. For every rake that strikes us brings with it a lesson, and lessons can be painful, my friend. These rakes whacking you in the face lessons are truly the seeds of wisdom."*

Ah, welcome! You made it! You've officially arrived at the self-help carnival, where the popcorn tastes like existential dread, the rides are powered by regret, and the prizes are—well—usually not what you were hoping for. But hey, at least you're here, which is more than we can say for the *version of you* who spent the last six months doomscrolling and justifying why "next Monday" would be the perfect time to start turning things around.

Let's be clear: I'm not here to sell you a pipe dream or a five-step program to achieve "success." That's not what this book is about. No one has time for another overly enthusiastic guru telling you that all your problems will be solved if you just visualize your success while sniffing organic eucalyptus oil and chanting affirmations in Sanskrit. (Spoiler alert: They won't be.)

Instead, this book is about figuring out why you keep stepping on metaphorical rakes. You know the ones. You're walking along, minding your own business, and *whack*! Right in the face. Every. Single. Time. The rake could be bad habits, toxic relationships, procrastination, or just the existential dread of being a person in the year 20-whatever-it-is-now. Sound familiar? Yeah, I thought so.

But here's the thing: You're not stupid, lazy, or broken. You're human. And being human means occasionally (okay, *frequently*) making bad choices, second-guessing yourself, and wondering if anyone else secretly has their life together while you're eating cereal for dinner in your pajamas. Newsflash: Nobody has it all figured out. Not even the people with matching throw pillows and alphabetized spice racks.

So, what's the plan here? Am I just going to roast you for 80 pages and call it a day? Tempting, but no. I'm here to help you *stop* stepping on those damn rakes. Not by making you perfect, but by helping you figure out how to get out of your own way long enough to move forward. It's about progress, not perfection. Baby steps, not moonwalks. And maybe a little bit of humor to keep things interesting because let's face it—if we can't laugh at ourselves, what's even the point?

Why Are You Here? (Besides the Obvious)

Let's talk about why you picked up this book—or, more likely, why you're scrolling through it on your phone while procrastinating on something important. You're here because you feel stuck. Maybe you're stuck in a job that sucks the soul out of you like a Dementor on caffeine. Maybe you're stuck in a cycle of bad habits, or you can't seem to make real progress on the things you care about. Or maybe you're just tired of stepping on the same damn rake repeatedly.

Whatever your reason, I want you to know this: Feeling stuck doesn't mean you're a failure. It just means you're human. And being human means, you've got a whole lot of messy, complicated, beautiful potential wrapped up in a package that occasionally eats cold pizza for breakfast.

Here's the deal: Change is hard. Not because you're incapable or unworthy, but because your brain is wired to resist it. It's called homeostasis—the tendency to stick to what feels familiar, even if what feels familiar is slowly making you miserable. Your brain doesn't care if you're happy; it cares if you're *comfortable*. And that's the first rake we need to deal with.

The First Rake: Comfort Is a Liar

Let's have an uncomfortable truth bomb, shall we? Comfort is a sneaky little liar. It whispers sweet nothings in your ear like, "Stay here where it's safe," and "Change is scary," and "You can always start tomorrow." And you listen because it's easier than facing the big, scary unknown.

But here's the catch: Comfort might feel good in the moment, but it's not where growth happens. Growth happens when you're willing to get a little uncomfortable—when you take risks, try new things, and push yourself just enough to break free from the rut you've been spinning your wheels in.

Think about it: Every major accomplishment in your life probably started with a moment of discomfort. Learning to ride a bike?

Terrifying. Asking someone out? Anxiety-inducing. Trying sushi for the first time? Highly questionable. But you did it, and you grew because of it. So, the next time comfort tries to convince you to stay where you are, I want you to picture it as an overly enthusiastic infomercial host. *"But wait! There's more! If you order now, you'll also get a lifetime of mediocrity and unfulfilled potential, free!"* Tempting, isn't it?

The Second Rake: Perfection Is Overrated

Ah, perfection—the gold-plated unicorn of self-improvement. We chase it because we think it'll make us happy, but here's the truth: Perfection is just a fancy word for procrastination.

Let me explain. When you tell yourself you can't start something until it's perfect—whether it's a project, a workout routine, or even just cleaning your kitchen—you're not aiming for excellence. You're stalling. You're giving yourself permission to stay stuck because deep down, you're afraid of failing.

But guess what? Failure is inevitable. It's also how you learn, grow, and eventually stop stepping on so many damn rakes. So, instead of aiming for perfection, aim for *progress*. Progress is messy, imperfect, and occasionally involves tripping over your own feet, but it's also the only way to get where you want to go.

The Third Rake: Motivation Is a Myth

You know those people who wake up at 5 a.m., go for a run, and drink kale smoothies before tackling their to-do list with the enthusiasm of a golden retriever? Yeah, me neither.

Here's the thing: Motivation is overrated. It's fleeting, unreliable, and about as trustworthy as a politician during campaign season. If you're waiting for motivation to strike before you act, you'll be waiting a long time.

What you need isn't motivation; it's momentum. Momentum doesn't rely on feelings or inspiration. It's about taking one small step, then another, and another, until you've built enough inertia to keep going even when you don't feel like it.

Start small. Stupidly small. Like, embarrassingly small. Want to start working out? Put on your sneakers. That's it. Want to write a novel? Open a blank document and type one sentence. Momentum doesn't care how you start—it just cares that you start.

The Fourth Rake: Comparing Yourself to Others

Oh, the joys of comparison. It's like playing a game of emotional roulette, except every slot on the wheel says, "you're not good enough." Social media doesn't help, of course. It's a highlight reel of other people's best moments, carefully curated to make you feel like you're failing in life.

But here's the truth: You're not competing with anyone else. The only person you need to compare yourself to is who you were yesterday. If you're even a little bit better, stronger, or kinder than you were the day before, you're winning.

The Fifth Rake: The Myth of "Having It All Together"

Let's dispel one of the biggest lies society has sold you: that there's a magical point in adulthood when you "figure it all out." Spoiler alert: that point doesn't exist. Nobody has it all together. Not your neighbor with the immaculate lawn, not your coworker with the color-coded planner, and not that influencer selling "positivity crystals" on Instagram.

Life is more like juggling flaming chainsaws than gracefully balancing a set of fine china. Some days you're on fire—in a good way. Other days, you're just *on fire*. And that's okay. Progress isn't about perfection or even consistency; it's about learning to roll with the punches (and maybe not setting yourself on fire too often).

So, stop aiming for the mythical "all together." Instead, aim for something more realistic, like "together enough that you don't cry in the grocery store parking lot this week." Trust me, that's winning.

Pause for Reflection: As you step into the world of this book, you're likely thinking, "Wait, rakes? What does stepping on rakes have to do with my life?" Well, let's take a moment to reflect. Life is full of rakes, isn't it? The missed opportunities, the mistakes, the "oops" moments that catch us off guard, often with painful consequences. We all step on rakes, metaphorically speaking. The question isn't whether we'll step on them—it's how we handle the strike when it happens. Do we fall down, defeated? Or do we stand up, laugh it off, and keep moving? Pause for a second and think about your rakes. What have they taught you? What will you choose to do differently next time? The true lesson in life isn't avoiding the rakes—it's learning how to dance with them, laughing at the absurdity, and using each one as a stepping stone to a better path.

Why This Book Won't Change Your Life (And Why That's a Good Thing)

Now, let's get one thing straight: this book won't magically fix all your problems. (What kind of rake would I be if I promised that?) Real, lasting change doesn't come from reading a book, watching a TED Talk, or binging a motivational YouTube playlist. It comes from doing the work—small, awkward, sometimes infuriating steps that eventually add up to something meaningful.

But here's the good news: this book *can* give you the tools to start. Think of it like a road map, except it's hand-drawn, a little sarcastic, and occasionally features stick figure doodles. It's not going to do the walking for you, but it can help you figure out which direction to head in—and maybe make the journey a little less miserable.

And let's be real: you're not here for a fairy tale. You're here because you're tired of stepping on rakes and ready to start moving forward, one small, imperfect step at a time.

What You'll Find in This Circus of a Book

Here's the deal: Each chapter is designed to tackle one of the biggest rakes in your life. We'll explore why it keeps smacking you in the face, how to avoid it in the future, and what to do when you inevitably trip over a different rake you didn't even see coming.

Expect sarcasm, humor, and the occasional heartfelt pep talk. (Yes, I *do* have a heart—it's just wrapped in a thick layer of snark.) You'll also find actionable advice, relatable stories, and maybe a few lightbulb moments along the way.

But fair warning: I'm not going to coddle you. Growth is uncomfortable, and sometimes you need a little tough love to get out of your own way. So, if you're looking for a sugar-coated, feel-good read, this isn't it. But if you're ready for a book that feels like a slightly unhinged but well-meaning friend yelling "YOU'VE GOT THIS!" while handing you a metaphorical rake shield, then you're in the right place.

A Quick Disclaimer (Because Lawyers Exist)

Before we dive in, let's address the obvious: I'm not a therapist, doctor, psychologist, life coach, or even a guru. I'm someone who's stepped on my fair share of rakes and lived to tell the tale. If you're dealing with serious mental health challenges, please seek professional help. This book isn't a substitute for therapy, it's more like a pep talk from that sarcastic friend who somehow always knows how to make you laugh when you're about to lose it.

Homework Time:

1. Identify Your Rakes: Think about the biggest obstacles or mistakes you've faced in your life. Write down a list of these

"rakes"—the moments when life caught you off guard and left you stunned. As you write, reflect on how these rakes have shaped you. Did they teach you patience? Resilience? A lesson in humility? Understanding the role of these rakes in your life is the first step in learning how to step around them more gracefully in the future.

2. Laugh at Your Mistakes: Find a recent mistake or failure and look at it with a sense of humor. Write about it, but instead of focusing on the negative, write a funny, exaggerated version of the story as if it were a comedy skit. How absurd was it that you stepped on that rake? This exercise helps take the sting out of mistakes and allows you to embrace the humor in life's challenges.

3. Prepare for the Next Rake: You know rakes are going to come, so let's get proactive. What tools can you develop to avoid stepping on the same rake again? Is it about being more mindful, practicing patience, or learning from your past mistakes? Write down one or two action steps that you will take to be more prepared for the rakes in your future.

End of Chapter Exercises:

1. Rake Reflection Journal: Each day for the next week, write about one "rake" you encountered—something that tripped you up, caught you off guard, or made you laugh. Reflect on how you handled it and what you could have done differently. Keep your focus on growth, not perfection.

2. Rake Awareness Practice: Whenever you find yourself rushing or feeling distracted, stop and take a breath. In that moment, ask yourself, "Is there a rake ahead that I'm not seeing?" Take a moment to slow down and notice your surroundings, whether it's your emotional state or physical environment. Awareness is key to avoiding future rakes.

3. Resilience Exercise: Think back to a time when stepping on a rake left you feeling embarrassed or discouraged. Now, reframe that experience as a moment of growth. What did you learn from it? How did it help you become more resilient? Write down how you can use that lesson in your life today, and how it has prepared you for future challenges.

Key Takeaways:

- Rakes Are Inevitable: Life is filled with rakes—mistakes, setbacks, and moments of failure. The key is not to avoid them but to learn how to navigate them with grace.

- Resilience is Built Through Rakes: Every time you step on a rake, you have an opportunity to rise stronger. The ability to bounce back from life's challenges is what builds resilience.

- Mistakes Are Learning Opportunities: Mistakes aren't failures; they are teachers in disguise. They show you where you need to grow and how you can do better next time.

- Awareness is Key: The more aware you are of your surroundings, your emotions, and your thoughts, the more likely you are to spot the rakes before they strike. Awareness allows you to step around them with ease.

- Humor is Your Ally: Laughter is a great way to reduce the sting of stepping on a rake. When you can laugh at yourself, you free yourself from the embarrassment or frustration that comes with failure.

Cheat Sheets & Recaps:

- The Power of Awareness: Pay attention to the rakes in your life—whether they're emotional, mental, or physical. The more aware you are, the less likely you are to step on them.

- Failure as Growth: Each rake represents a lesson. Embrace your failures, learn from them, and grow stronger.
- Resilience Is a Choice: Resilience is not something you're born with; it's a skill you develop by facing adversity and learning to rise again.
- Humor Makes Life Easier: When you stop taking yourself too seriously, the rakes become less intimidating. Laugh at life's mishaps, and you'll learn to handle them with grace.
- Let the Rakes Teach You: Don't avoid the rakes—let them teach you how to navigate life with more awareness, patience, and resilience.

Kenism: *"What you need to understand is that the garden is not without its challenges, and neither is your life. It will not always be a smooth path. There will be rakes, unexpected obstacles, and stumbles. But these rakes—they are not the end of the road. They are not setbacks. They are what make you pay attention. Life will never ask for your permission before presenting a challenge, but it will always teach you something. Each step forward, no matter how small or painful, it shapes your journey. So, embrace the rakes. Embrace the pain. And let it teach you the art of moving forward with more clarity, more understanding, and with a touch of humor."*

Chapter Conclusion: Let's Get This Show on the Road

Alright, enough with the warm-up. You're here because you're ready to stop stepping on rakes and start living a life that doesn't feel like one long blooper reel. That doesn't mean everything will suddenly become easy or that you won't face setbacks along the way. You will. But it *does* mean you're capable of moving forward, even if it's one small, awkward step at a time.

So, take a deep breath, grab your metaphorical rake shield, and let's get started. The first step is always the hardest, but you've already taken it by picking up this book. And for that, I'm ridiculously proud of you. Now, let's go kick some rake-ass.

And with that, the circus begins. Get ready to laugh, learn, and maybe even surprise yourself along the way. Let's do this!

TL;DR: Life is filled with rakes, those moments when we trip, fall, and fail. But instead of fearing them, we should learn from them. Each rake is an opportunity to build resilience, grow stronger, and navigate life with greater awareness. When we stop rushing and start embracing life's challenges with humor and patience, we stop stepping on rakes and start dancing through life.

Notes:

Chapter 1: Congratulations, You're a Hot Mess (But Fixable)

Kenism: *"In the pursuit of a purposeful life, the path we walk often seems scattered with distractions. We search for the right way, yet our eyes are so fixed on the goal that we fail to see the rake lying in wait. The question is not why the rake appears on the path, but rather how we respond when it strikes us. In a way, the rake is your friend. It brings your attention back to the present. It reminds you that the path to clarity is not paved with ease, but with awareness of where you step. Your true growth is in noticing the rakes before they strike, in understanding that they are not there to harm you, but to awaken you."*

You've made it to Chapter 1. Congrats! That's already more progress than most people make. Seriously, how many times have you bought a book like this, read the intro, then promptly used it as a coaster for your coffee mug of despair? (Don't lie—we've all been there.)

But this time it is different. Why? Because this time, you're not just reading; you're *doing*. Or at least you're *thinking* about doing, which is practically the same thing when you're starting from zero. So, let's dive in and address the big, messy elephant in the room: You're a hot mess.

Now, before you get offended and chuck this book across the room, let me clarify: being a hot mess is not a bad thing. It's just a thing. A human thing. We all have days (or decades) when we feel like we're held together with duct tape and a prayer. The key is not to let the mess define you. Instead, you're going to learn how to embrace it, laugh at it, and then slowly, methodically clean it up—one metaphorical pizza box at a time.

What Does "Hot Mess" Even Mean?

Let's break it down. A hot mess isn't just someone who leaves laundry in the washer until it smells like a wet dog. It's someone who feels like they're spinning plates while riding a unicycle on a tightrope—except the plates are on fire, the unicycle has a flat tire, and the tightrope is fraying. Sound familiar?

Being a hot mess is about more than just forgetting to pay your electric bill or eating a questionable amount of cereal straight from the box. It's about feeling like you're constantly two steps behind where you *should* be, whatever that means. It's the anxiety of trying to hold it all together while secretly wondering if everyone else has access to some kind of life cheat code you missed out on.

Spoiler alert: They don't.

Here's the truth: Nobody has their life perfectly together. Not your Instagram-perfect coworker, not the mom at the park with matching kid outfits, and definitely not Jeff Bezos (have you seen his laugh?). Everyone's a hot mess in their own way. The difference is that some people have learned to manage the mess, while others are still flailing around trying to figure out which end of the broom to hold.

The Good News: You're Not Alone

One of the worst things about being a hot mess is feeling like you're the only one who hasn't cracked the adulting code. But let me tell you a little secret: the entire world is full of people who feel like they're barely scraping by.

Think about it. How many times have you seen someone pull up to the drive-thru in their pajamas at 3 p.m.? Or overheard a stranger in Target muttering to themselves about how they can't remember why they're there? That's your tribe. These are your people.

You're not broken. You're just part of a species that invented Wi-Fi but still hasn't figured out how to microwave a burrito evenly. And that's okay.

The Even Better News: You're Fixable

Here's the thing: being a hot mess isn't a permanent state. It's more like a season—a really chaotic, confusing season, like winter but with fewer snowflakes and more existential dread. And just like seasons, it can change. You *can* learn to manage the chaos, find your footing, and create a life that feels less like a constant dumpster fire and more like a cozy campfire (complete with s'mores, obviously).

But first, you need to accept one fundamental truth: Change is possible, but it's also work. Real, messy, uncomfortable work. And that's where most people get stuck—they want the results without the effort. But you're not most people. You're here, you're reading this book, and that means you're ready to roll up your sleeves and get to work.

Step 1: Own Your Hot Mess Status

The first step to fixing any problem is admitting you have one. So, say it with me: "I'm a hot mess." There. Doesn't that feel better?

Now, let's get specific. What does your hot mess look like? Is it a mountain of unfinished projects? A calendar so overbooked it makes airline schedules look chill? Or maybe it's just a general sense of blah, like you're stuck in quicksand and can't quite figure out how to escape.

Whatever your personal brand of messiness is, I want you to own it. Write it down if you have to. List every chaotic, embarrassing, or frustrating thing that's weighing you down. Not to shame yourself, but to get it all out in the open. Think of it like Marie Kondo-ing your brain—acknowledge the mess, thank it for its service, and then prepare to let it go.

Step 2: Stop Should-ing All Over Yourself

One of the biggest traps hot messes fall into is the "should" spiral. *"I should have my life together by now." "I should be more productive." "I should stop eating Taco Bell at 11 p.m."*

Let me tell you something: "Should" is a toxic little word. It's not helpful. It's not motivating. All it does is pile guilt and shame onto your already full plate, and that's the last thing you need.

So, here's your new mantra: Stop should-ing all over yourself. Instead of focusing on what you think you *should* do, focus on what you *can* do. Forget about the big picture for now—what's one small, manageable thing you can do today to move in the right direction? Maybe it's sending that one email you've been avoiding. Maybe it's finally putting away the laundry. Whatever it is, start small.

Step 3: Embrace the Power of "Good Enough"

Let's talk about perfectionism. If you're a hot mess, chances are you're also a recovering perfectionist. You set impossibly high standards for yourself, and then beat yourself up when you inevitably fall short. It's a vicious cycle, and it's time to break it.

Here's the deal: Perfection is overrated. Nobody's perfect, and striving for perfection is just another way of setting yourself up to fail. So, instead of aiming for perfect, aim for "good enough."

Good enough means getting the job done without obsessing over every little detail. It means accepting that sometimes "finished" is better than "flawless." And it means giving yourself permission to be human, mistakes and all.

Step 4: Learn to Laugh at Yourself

Life is ridiculous. The sooner you learn to laugh at it—and yourself—the easier it becomes. So, the next time you find yourself spiraling into hot mess territory, try to see the humor in it.

Burnt dinner? Congratulations, you've invented charcoal-based cuisine. Forgot your friend's birthday? Oops, time to become the world's greatest belated gift giver. Lost your car keys again? Hey, at least you're consistent.

Humor doesn't fix the mess, but it makes it a lot easier to handle. Plus, laughing at yourself is way more fun than crying into your fourth cup of coffee.

Pause for Reflection

Welcome to the start of your journey! Alright, let's take a breath. You've just acknowledged your hot mess status, ditched the toxic "shoulds," embraced "good enough," and started laughing at your own ridiculousness. That's a lot for one chapter, and you're crushing it so far. In this chapter, we took a thorough analysis into the metaphor of life's rakes—those obstacles and challenges that trip us up when we least expect them. But here's the real question: What did you learn about yourself in the process?

Reflect for a moment—think about a time when you stepped on a metaphorical rake. What was it? Did it knock you down? Or did you rise up, brush yourself off, and keep walking? In the first half of this book, we've explored the idea that these rakes aren't here to break us; they're here to teach us. They're part of the journey, not the destination. Pause and reflect on your rakes. What do they reveal about where you are on your path? And how can you use these rakes to move forward with more awareness and grace?

But don't get too comfortable. We've got plenty more rakes to deal with, and the next one is a doozy. For now, give yourself a pat on the back, maybe a snack (preferably one that doesn't come from a vending machine), and get ready to dive into the next step of your journey.

Step 5: Break Up With Your Inner Critic

Now let's talk about the little voice in your head—the one that whispers things like, *"You're not good enough," "You'll never figure this out,"* and *"Remember that time you embarrassed yourself in seventh grade?"* Yeah, that jerk needs to go.

Your inner critic is like the world's worst roommate. It eats your confidence, hogs your mental space, and leaves negativity all over the place. And yet, you let it live rent-free in your head. Why? Because somewhere along the way, you started believing it.

Here's the truth: Your inner critic isn't your friend. It's a self-sabotaging goblin that thrives on your insecurities. So, it's time to kick it to the curb.

Every time that voice pops up, I want you to challenge it. Ask yourself, *"Is this actually true, or is it just fear talking?"* Most of the time, it's fear. And fear is about as reliable as a $5 umbrella in a hurricane.

To take it a step further, give your inner critic a ridiculous name. Something like "Negative Nancy," "Judgey McJudgeface," or "Kevin." Then, when it starts spewing its nonsense, you can roll your eyes and say, *"Oh, shut up, Kevin."* It sounds silly, but it works.

Step 6: Build a Toolbox for Your Hot Mess Moments

Let's face it: Life is going to throw you curveballs. No matter how much progress you make, there will be days when everything feels like it's falling apart. And that's okay. The key is to have a toolbox of strategies to help you handle those moments without completely losing your cool.

Here are a few tools to get you started:

- **The 5-Minute Rule**: When you're overwhelmed, commit to doing *just five minutes* of whatever task is stressing you out. Most of the time, once you start, you'll keep going. But even if you don't, five minutes is still progress.

- **The Brain Dump**: Grab a piece of paper and write down every single thing that's cluttering your mind. Don't worry about organizing it—just get it all out. Once it's on paper, it's easier to prioritize and tackle.

- **The Emergency Dance Party**: Feeling stuck? Blast your favorite song and dance like a lunatic for three minutes. It's impossible to stay stressed when you're channeling your inner Beyoncé.

- **The Magic of Saying "No"**: Repeat after me: *"No" is a complete sentence.* You don't have to say yes to every request, invitation, or obligation. Protecting your time and energy is one of the most powerful things you can do.

Step 7: Celebrate the Small Wins

Hot messes have a tendency to focus on what's wrong instead of what's right. You spend so much time beating yourself up for not being perfect that you forget to celebrate the little victories along the way.

Did you get out of bed today? Victory. Did you tackle a task you've been avoiding for weeks? Double victory. Did you remember to eat a vegetable? You deserve a freaking medal.

Small wins add up. They're like breadcrumbs leading you out of the forest of chaos. So, every time you accomplish something—no matter how small—take a moment to acknowledge it. High-five yourself in the mirror, do a little happy dance, or reward yourself with something you love (yes, snacks count).

The Hot Mess Anthem: Progress, Not Perfection

By now, you've probably noticed a recurring theme in this chapter: progress, not perfection. It's the mantra of hot messes everywhere, and for good reason.

Perfection is a myth. It's the unattainable standard that keeps you stuck in a cycle of procrastination, self-doubt, and frustration. But progress? Progress is real. It's tangible. It's what happens when you take one small step, then another, and another, until suddenly you're miles away from where you started.

So, let go of the idea that you need to have it all figured out. You don't. All you need to do is keep moving forward, one imperfect step at a time.

Your Hot Mess Homework

Before we wrap up this chapter, let's put some of these ideas into action. Don't worry—it's not graded, and there's no deadline. This is just a chance to start building momentum.

1. **List Your Rakes**: Write down the top three things that are making you feel like a hot mess right now. Be specific.

2. **Pick One Small Step**: Choose one tiny, manageable action you can take today to address one of those rakes. Remember, we're aiming for embarrassingly small.

3. **Celebrate a Win**: Think of one thing you've done recently—no matter how small—that deserves celebration. Then actually celebrate it. (Yes, ice cream counts.)

4. **Tell Kevin to Shut Up**: The next time your inner critic starts mouthing off, give it a name and tell it to pipe down. Bonus points if you do it out loud.

Optional Homework Time:

1. **Identify Your Current Rakes:** Think about one area in your life where you keep tripping up. It could be a habit, a goal you're pursuing, or a challenge you keep facing. Write it down. Now, consider what might be causing you to step on that particular rake. Is it a lack of awareness? A habit of rushing? Reflect on what you can do differently next time to avoid it—or, at the very least, learn from it. The goal here is to recognize where you're prone to stepping on rakes and come up with a strategy to handle them with more clarity.

2. **Rake Reframing:** Think of a recent failure, big or small, and reframe it. What did you learn from the experience? How could this failure actually be an opportunity for growth? Write down what you would do differently, and how you can use this lesson to avoid a similar rake in the future. The key here is to shift from seeing failure as a setback to seeing it as a stepping stone.

3. **Set an Intention for Awareness:** The next time you face a decision or challenge, set an intention to be fully present. This is your moment to spot the rake before it strikes. Write down one small action you can take today to become more aware and more mindful of where you're stepping. Awareness is the first step in avoiding future rakes.

End of Chapter Exercises:

1. **Mindfulness Walk:** Go for a walk and take note of everything around you. Don't let your mind wander—stay present in the moment. Pay attention to the ground beneath your feet, your surroundings, and your breath. The goal of this exercise is to train yourself to stay aware, which will help you spot the rakes in your life before they catch you off guard. Write down any thoughts or insights you had during the walk.

2. **Reflective Journaling:** Spend 10 minutes reflecting on a past "rake moment" where you tripped up. Write about how you felt in the moment and how you handled it. What were your immediate reactions? Now, imagine how you could have responded differently. This exercise helps you recognize patterns in your behavior, and over time, it will help you avoid making the same mistakes.

3. **Proactive Rake Strategy:** Identify a recurring challenge in your life. Write down a specific action plan for how you can approach it differently the next time you encounter it. This could involve slowing down, practicing mindfulness, or creating a new strategy for handling the situation. The goal is to be proactive about dealing with your rakes and preventing them from tripping you up in the future.

Key Takeaways:

- **Life is Full of Rakes:** The key is not to avoid them, but to learn from them. Every failure, setback, or challenge is an opportunity to grow.

- **Awareness Is the First Step:** The more aware you are of your surroundings and your inner thoughts, the more likely you are to see the rakes coming and avoid them.

- **Failure Is a Teacher:** Every time you step on a rake, it's a lesson. What did you learn? How can you grow from the experience? View each failure as a steppingstone, not a setback.

- **You Control How You Respond:** The rakes aren't what determine your journey. How you respond to them is what shapes your path. Stay grounded, learn from each misstep, and keep moving forward with resilience.

- **Rakes Are Opportunities for Growth:** Don't fear the rakes in your life. They are there to teach you, and with each lesson, you move closer to becoming the best version of yourself.

Cheat Sheets & Recaps:

- **Awareness First, Then Action:** Pay attention to where you step. The more aware you are of the present moment, the easier it will be to avoid stepping on metaphorical rakes.

- **Failure Is Not the End:** View failure as a chance to learn. With each setback, ask yourself, "What can I learn from this?" and move forward with a new perspective.

- **Mindfulness = Awareness:** Slowing down and being present in the moment helps you notice the rakes ahead of time. Use mindfulness as your tool for greater clarity.

- **Resilience Is Key:** When you do step on a rake, don't stay down. Rise, learn, and keep going. Your ability to bounce back is what matters.

- **Plan:** The more proactive you are about identifying the rakes in your life, the less likely you are to trip on them. Plan for how to navigate challenges before they arise.

Kenism: *"You see, the moment you realize that the rake is not an enemy, but a guide, you begin to change your relationship with life's challenges. The path will still have rakes, and yes, you will trip. But now, each time, you rise with greater awareness. The mistake is not in stepping on the rake, but in failing to learn from it. So, move forward, with your eyes open to the rakes and your heart willing to learn from each misstep. Life will bring its challenges, but it's your reaction that will define your journey. What's important is not avoiding the rake, but what you do when it strikes."*

Final Thoughts:

Congratulations, you've made it through Chapter 1! That's already more than most people accomplish when they're feeling stuck. But this is just the beginning. You've acknowledged your hot mess status, embraced the power of "good enough," and started building your toolbox for handling life's chaos.

The road ahead won't be perfect—spoiler alert: you're going to trip over a few more rakes along the way. But that's okay. Because now you've got the tools, the mindset, and maybe even a little bit of momentum to keep moving forward.

So, take a deep breath, give yourself a well-deserved pat on the back, and get ready for the next chapter. We've got plenty more rakes to tackle, but for now, just remember you're a hot mess, but you're also fixable. And that's something worth celebrating.

TL;DR: Life is full of rakes, but they aren't obstacles, they're opportunities for growth. The key is awareness. By staying present and mindful, you can spot the rakes before they strike. When you do trip, remember: it's not the rake that matters, but how you handle it. Every failure is a lesson, and every lesson brings you one step closer to mastering life's path. So, take a deep breath, slow down, and keep moving forward with greater clarity and resilience.

Stop Stepping on Rakes: Laugh at Your Mistakes, Learn from Them, and Keep Moving Forward

Chapter 2: Why Nothing Has Worked (Yet)

Kenism: *"Imagine you are walking down a road, blissfully unaware of the rakes scattered in your path. But then, life hits you, not once, not twice, but several times—each strike a reminder of your own blind spots. You see, awareness is not something you achieve by looking out for the rake. It is achieved by being present enough to recognize the spaces between the rakes—the moments where clarity arises. It is not the rakes themselves that shape your destiny, but your ability to see them, to understand them, and to move around them with grace."*

Welcome to Chapter 2, where we dive into the question you've been asking yourself every time you've tried to change your life, only to end up face-planting into the same old habits: *"Why hasn't anything worked?"*

You've tried everything, right? The morning routines, the self-help books, the Pinterest vision boards, the guided meditations with a guy named Trevor who speaks in a voice so soothing it's mildly suspicious. And yet, here you are, feeling stuck and wondering if you're just destined to live in a never-ending cycle of trying and failing.

Good news: It's not you. Well, not entirely. The truth is the systems you've been relying on are broken—or at least not designed for the beautiful chaos that is *you*. So, let's dissect the problem, figure out what's been holding you back, and start building a foundation for change that works this time.

The First Problem: The Quick Fix Trap

Ah, the allure of the quick fix. Who among us hasn't fallen for the promise of overnight success? "Lose 20 pounds in two weeks!" "Transform your mindset with this one simple trick!" "Become a millionaire by doing nothing except manifesting your dreams while eating Cheetos!"

Here's the thing about quick fixes: they're like duct tape on a leaky pipe. Sure, they might work for a little while, but eventually, the pressure builds, the tape gives out, and you're left with an even bigger mess.

Real, lasting change doesn't happen overnight. It's slow, messy, and often feels like you're trying to untangle a ball of Christmas lights while wearing oven mitts. But that's okay, because the slow and steady approach is the one that sticks.

So, the next time you're tempted by a quick fix, remember this: If it sounds too good to be true, it probably is. And if it involves anything called a "detox tea," just run.

The Second Problem: The Motivation Myth

Let's talk about motivation. You've probably been told that it's the key to success—that all you need to do is *get motivated* and everything will magically fall into place. But here's the truth: Motivation is about as reliable as a 1998 printer. It works when it feels like it, which is almost never.

Motivation is fickle. It shows up when you're excited about a new idea but disappears the second things get hard. That's why relying on motivation to drive changes are like trying to power your car with fairy dust—it's just not sustainable.

What you need instead is a system—a set of habits and routines that keep you moving forward even when you don't feel like it. Systems don't rely on willpower or inspiration; they rely on consistency. And consistency, my friend, is the unsung hero of progress.

The Third Problem: All-or-Nothing Thinking

Oh, all-or-nothing thinking, you cruel mistress. This is the mindset that says, *"If I can't do it perfectly, I might as well not do it at all."*

You miss one workout and decide your entire fitness journey is ruined. You eat one donut and figure you might as well devour the whole box. You skip one day of journaling and suddenly you're questioning your entire existence. Sound familiar?

Here's a radical idea: You don't have to be perfect to make progress. In fact, the most successful people in the world are the ones who screw up, learn from it, and keep going. So, the next time you catch yourself falling into the all-or-nothing trap, remember this: Doing *something* is always better than doing *nothing*.

The Fourth Problem: Unrealistic Expectations

Let's be real: Your expectations are probably a little… ambitious. You decide to overhaul your entire life in one week—quit sugar, start working out, meditate daily, and learn Mandarin. By day three, you're stress-eating Oreos and wondering why you thought this was a good idea.

The problem isn't you; it's your expectations. Change doesn't happen in giant leaps; it happens in tiny, incremental steps. So, instead of trying to do everything at once, pick one small, manageable goal and focus on that. Master it, then move on to the next thing.

Remember: Progress isn't about speed; it's about direction. As long as you're moving forward, you're winning.

The Fifth Problem: Ignoring the Why

Let's get deep for a second. Why do you want to change? No, really—*why?*

If your answer is something vague like, *"I want to be happy"* or *"I want to be successful,"* that's not going to cut it. You need to dig deeper. What does happiness look like for you? What does success feel like? Why do these things matter?

Understanding your "why" is crucial because it gives you a reason to keep going when things get tough. It's the anchor that keeps you grounded, the fuel that keeps you moving, and the light at the end of the tunnel when you're tempted to give up.

So, take some time to figure out your "why." Write it down. Make it specific. And keep it somewhere you'll see it often, like your bathroom mirror or the lock screen on your phone.

The Sixth Problem: The Dopamine Trap

Let's talk science for a minute. Your brain is a dopamine junkie. It loves quick hits of pleasure, which is why it's so easy to scroll through TikTok for hours but so hard to focus on writing that report for work.

The problem is, the things that give you those quick dopamine hits—social media, junk food, Netflix binges—don't actually make you happy in the long run. They're like sugar: they give you a temporary high, followed by a crash that leaves you feeling worse than before.

If you want to create real, lasting change, you need to rewire your brain to crave the *right* kinds of rewards. Start by replacing some of your dopamine traps with activities that align with your goals. For example, instead of mindlessly scrolling, try reading a book or going for a walk. It won't feel as instantly gratifying at first, but over time, your brain will start to associate these activities with pleasure.

The Seventh Problem: The Fear of Failure

Ah, failure. The big, scary monster hiding under the bed of every self-improvement journey. Nobody likes to fail, but here's the thing: Failure isn't the enemy. It's the teacher.

Every successful person you admire has failed—probably more times than they can count. The difference is, they didn't let failure stop them. They learned from it, adapted, and kept going.

So, instead of fearing failure, start embracing it. Celebrate your mistakes as evidence that you're trying. Because the only true failure is giving up entirely.

Pause for Reflection

Alright, let's take stock of where we are. You've learned why quick fixes, motivation, and all-or-nothing thinking don't work. You've tackled unrealistic expectations, uncovered the importance of your "why," and started rewiring your brain to crave the right kinds of rewards. Not bad for one chapter, huh?

Now that we've established the rakes in life, it's time to dig a little deeper into the true power of awareness. It's one thing to step on a rake and learn from it—but the real magic happens when you can see the rakes before they even have the chance to strike. Awareness isn't just about avoiding mistakes; it's about understanding where you are, where you've been, and where you're going.

Think about the times in your life when you were most "aware"—when you were fully present and in tune with your surroundings. How did that awareness impact your choices? Pause for a moment and reflect: What would it feel like if you were more aware in your day-today life? If you could see the rakes, not as obstacles, but as opportunities to steer your path with greater intention?

But don't get too comfortable—we've got more to cover. The next step is figuring out how to acquire all this knowledge and put it into action. And trust me, *THAT* is where the magic happens.

The Eighth Problem: Your Environment Is Working Against You

Let's talk about your environment for a second. I'm not just talking about the clutter in your living room (though, yes, that pile of laundry staring at you from the couch isn't helping). I mean the broader environment you've built around yourself: the people you spend time with, the habits you reinforce, and the spaces where you spend your days.

Your environment can be your greatest ally or your sneakiest saboteur. If you're trying to eat healthier but your pantry looks like the snack aisle at 7-Eleven, guess what? You're setting yourself up to fail. If you're trying to get focused work done but you're sitting in front of the TV with your phone in hand, yeah, good luck with that.

Here's the deal: Willpower is overrated. What really matters is creating an environment that makes it easier to succeed and harder to fail. Think of it like baby-proofing your life—not because you're a baby, but because you're human, and humans are naturally drawn to the path of least resistance.

Want to work out more? Lay out your gym clothes the night before. Want to read more books? Put them where you can see them (and maybe delete that Kindle app shortcut next to TikTok). Your environment should work *with* you, not against you.

The Ninth Problem: You're Doing It Alone

Here's an unpopular truth: You can't do this on your own. Nobody can.

The self-made person is a myth—a lovely, romantic myth that sounds great in commencement speeches but doesn't hold up in real life. Every success story you've ever heard is built on a foundation of support, whether it's family, friends, mentors, or even strangers cheering you on from the sidelines.

So, why are you trying to do this alone? If you're serious about making lasting changes, you need a support system. That doesn't mean you need a full entourage or a life coach named Chad, but you do need people who believe in you, hold you accountable, and maybe even tell you to snap out of it when you're having a pity party.

Your support system can take many forms: a workout buddy, a mentor, an online community, or even a snarky book like this one (hi, it's me). The point is, you're stronger with allies in your corner. So, if you've been isolating yourself, it's time to reach out.

The Tenth Problem: You're Afraid of Success

Okay, this one might sound counterintuitive, but hear me out: Sometimes the thing holding you back isn't fear of failure, it's fear of *success.*

Success means change. It means stepping into the unknown, taking on new responsibilities, and maybe even redefining who you are. And that's terrifying. Because what if you succeed and then realize you're still not happy? Or what if you succeed and suddenly people expect more from you?

Here's the thing: Fear of success is normal, but it's also self-sabotage. It keeps you stuck in a safe, familiar place, even when that place isn't serving you. The only way to overcome it is to face it head-on.

Ask yourself: *What am I really afraid of?* Write it down. Then ask yourself: *What's the worst that could happen if I succeed? And what's the best that could happen?* Take your time to think of multiple options. You soon discover that your "doom thinking" isn't true, that you will be okay and to think differently. Spoiler alert: In reality, the best-case scenario is probably way better than the worst-case scenario is bad.

The Solution: Start Small, Start Now

If you've made it this far, you're probably wondering, *"Okay, but what do I actually do?"* Don't worry, I'm not about to hit you with some vague motivational platitudes. Instead, I'm going to give you a simple, actionable plan:

1. **Pick One Thing**: Forget about overhauling your entire life. Choose one small, specific area to focus on—something that feels manageable, not overwhelming.

2. **Break It Down**: Take that one thing and break it into the smallest possible steps. If your goal is to start working out, your first step might be putting on your sneakers. That's it.

3. **Set a Timer**: Commit to working on your goal for just five minutes. No pressure, no big expectations, just five minutes. Once you've started, you'll often find it easier to keep going.

4. **Celebrate Progress**: Every step forward is a win, no matter how small. Treat yourself like you'd treat a friend—acknowledge the effort, not just the outcome.

The Power of Consistency

Here's the not-so-sexy truth about success: It's boring. It's not about dramatic transformations or grand gestures; it's about showing up every day and doing the work, even when you don't feel like it.

Consistency is the secret sauce. It's what separates the people who achieve their goals from the ones who give up halfway through. And the best part? You don't have to be perfect to be consistent. Missing a day doesn't mean you've failed; it just means you're human. The key is to get back on track and keep moving forward.

Homework Time: Let's Get Practical

By now, your brain is probably buzzing with ideas, insights, and maybe even a touch of existential dread. That's okay—it means you're paying attention. But knowledge without action is just trivia, so let's turn all this theory into practice.

Here's your homework for this chapter:

1. **Identify Your Biggest Rake**: What's the one thing that's been holding you back the most? Write it down.

2. **Plan Your First Step**: What's one tiny, actionable step you can take today to start tackling that rake? Remember, smaller is better.

3. **Find Your "Why"**: Take five minutes to write down why this goal matters to you. Be specific.

4. **Rearrange Your Environment**: Make one small change to your environment that supports your goal.

5. **Recruit a Buddy**: Reach out to someone who can support you, hold you accountable, or just cheer you on.

Optional Homework Time:

1. **Spot the Rake Before It Strikes:** For the next week, take one situation in your life where you tend to rush or react without thinking. It could be an everyday interaction or a bigger decision. Before acting, take a pause—count to five, breathe, and assess the situation. What rakes do you see? Write down how taking a pause changed your reaction and how it helped you avoid potential pitfalls.

2. **Create a "Rake Alert" System:** Set a reminder for yourself at least once a day (preferably when you're most likely to rush or get distracted). When the reminder goes off, take a few minutes to become fully present. Take deep breaths, and check in with your thoughts, emotions, and surroundings. Notice any rakes lying around you that you might not have seen before. Write down your observations each time. The goal is to train yourself to become more aware and proactive.

3. **Awareness Challenge:** Choose one activity you do regularly (e.g., eating, walking, or driving) and commit to doing it with full awareness for the next week. Focus entirely on the task at hand—no distractions, no multitasking. Write down your thoughts and feelings as you experience this heightened awareness. What did you notice that you usually miss? This exercise will help you practice mindfulness and improve your awareness throughout the day.

End of Chapter Exercises:

1. **The Power of the Pause:** The next time you're about to decide, big or small, take a pause. Close your eyes, take three deep breaths, and bring your full awareness to the present moment. Think about the potential rakes in the situation and assess how you want to proceed. Write your experience afterward, noting how much more in control you felt by taking that extra moment to reflect.

2. **Awareness Mapping:** Take a piece of paper and draw a map of your day—literally or figuratively. What activities take up most of your time? Where do you feel the most distracted? Where do you feel present and focused? Reflect on where you tend to "step on the rakes." Highlight the areas in your life where you want to increase your awareness and make conscious choices. This exercise helps you visualize the places where awareness will make the most difference.

3. **Gratitude Practice:** Spend five minutes each day noticing the small, often-overlooked details of your life that you're grateful for. This could be something as simple as the feeling of sunlight on your skin, a cup of coffee in the morning, taking your pet for a walk or playing with them at home, or even the kind smile of a stranger. By practicing daily awareness, you cultivate gratitude, which strengthens your mindfulness muscles for spotting rakes.

Key Takeaways:

- **Awareness Is the First Line of Defense:** The more aware you are, the more likely you are to spot potential obstacles or challenges before they trip you up. Avoiding unnecessary pain hinges on awareness.

- **Avoiding pain isn't awareness's only purpose; it's about living presently, noticing life's beauty, opportunities, and lessons.** It's a mindset, not just a reaction.

- **The Power of Pausing:** Taking a moment to pause and assess your thoughts, emotions, and surroundings helps you make better, more intentional decisions. It's in that pause that true awareness blossoms.

- **Awareness Creates Choice:** When you're aware, you have the power to choose. You can decide how to respond to a situation rather than reacting impulsively. Awareness gives you control.

- **Being Present Changes Everything:** The more present you are in each moment, the less likely you are to miss the subtle cues and opportunities that can help you avoid the rakes. Through awareness, the ordinary becomes extraordinary.

Cheat Sheets & Recaps:

- **Your superpower is awareness: Being present minimizes mishaps.** Awareness helps you navigate life's challenges with greater ease and clarity.

- **The Pause Is Key:** Before reacting, pause. In that pause, you have the space to make a mindful, intentional decision. The more you practice this pause, the easier it becomes to handle life's challenges with grace.

- **Mindfulness Leads to Better Choices:** Living with intention means slowing down and being present. When you practice mindfulness, you make better choices, avoiding unnecessary mistakes or rakes along the way.

- **Spotting the Rake Early Is the Key:** By being aware of your thoughts, feelings, and surroundings, you can see potential rakes before they spring up. Awareness helps you prepare for what's ahead.

- **Practice Makes Presence:** The more you practice being present in everyday moments, the more naturally it will come to you when you need it most. Practice mindfulness to increase your awareness.

Kenism: *"As you become more aware, the world does not necessarily change, but you do. The rakes, once obstacles, become opportunities for growth. They show you where you need to slow down, where you need to sharpen your focus. So, stop rushing forward, trying to avoid every rake. Instead, start looking for the gaps between them, for the places where clarity resides. Life is a dance between action and awareness, and once you start to see the rakes for what they are—teachers, not enemies—you will navigate the path with a steady, unshakable mind."*

Final Thoughts

Congratulations, you've just tackled one of the biggest questions in self-improvement: *Why hasn't anything worked yet?* More importantly, you've started building the foundation for change that actually sticks.

It's not going to be easy, and it's definitely not going to be quick. But with the right mindset, the right systems, and a little bit of patience, you *can* create a life that feels less like a series of failed experiments and more like a work in progress you're proud of.

So, take a deep breath, give yourself a high five (yes, really), and get ready for the next chapter. Because the journey is just beginning, and you're already doing better than you think.

TL;DR: Awareness is the key to avoiding life's rakes. By slowing down, pausing, and being present in the moment, you can spot the obstacles ahead and make better choices. In this chapter, we learned how to train our minds to become more aware, to make the pause a habit, and to navigate life with greater intention and clarity. The more aware you are, the less likely you are to trip up. It's time to take control, be present, and avoid those rakes with ease.

Notes:

Chapter 3: Baby Steps for Grown-Ups

Kenism: *"Fear is a natural companion to life. It's the voice inside us that warns, 'Don't walk too fast, don't make a move, or you might step on the rake!' But fear, much like the rake, is a tool. A tool that serves you only if you use it wisely. If fear stops you from moving, it has become your master. If you use it as a teacher, it will guide you to deeper awareness. Don't avoid fear; instead, confront it, move forward, and discover what lies beyond the pain.*

Congratulations my friend, you've officially made it to Chapter 3. You're on a roll! You're like the little engine that could, except instead of chugging along on pure optimism, you're fueled by coffee, existential dread, and maybe a sprinkle of spite for all the doubters who didn't think you'd make it this far. (Spoiler alert: They were wrong. You *ARE* killing it.)

Now, let's talk about the secret to making a real lasting change: *baby steps.*

I know what you're thinking. *"Baby steps? Really? I'm a grown adult. I've paid taxes, cried in a Walmart parking lot, and stayed up until 2 a.m. Googling weird health symptoms. I don't need baby steps."*

But here's the thing: You absolutely do. And that's OKAY!

Why Baby Steps Work (Even If They Sound Ridiculous)

Let's start with some real talk: Change is hard. Like, "trying to assemble IKEA furniture without instructions" hard. If you try to tackle everything at once, you're going to get overwhelmed, frustrated, and probably end up stress-eating an entire box of Oreos.

Baby steps, on the other hand, are manageable. They're small enough that they don't set off your brain's internal "This is too hard; let's quit!" alarm, but meaningful enough that they move you closer to your goal.

Think of it like climbing a mountain. If you stare up at the peak, you're going to freak out and convince yourself it's impossible. But if you focus on putting one foot in front of the other, suddenly it doesn't seem so daunting. Baby steps are the foundation of progress, and progress is how you win the long game.

The Psychology of Small Wins

Here's a fun fact: Your brain loves winning. Every time you accomplish something—even something small—it releases a hit of dopamine; the feel-good chemical that makes you want to keep going.

That's why breaking your goals into tiny, bite-sized pieces is so effective. Each baby step you complete is like a little win for your brain. It doesn't matter if the step is as small as drinking a glass of water or sending a single email. A win is a win, and your brain is going to reward you for it.

So, instead of trying to overhaul your entire life in one go, focus on racking up as many small wins as possible. It's like a video game, but instead of collecting coins or slaying dragons, you're building momentum and slaying your own self-doubt.

How to Take Your First Baby Step

Okay, so you're sold on the idea of baby steps. Great! Now comes the fun part: figuring out where to start.

Here's the golden rule of baby steps: Start stupidly small. I'm talking so small that it feels almost laughable. Why? Because small steps are easy to commit to, and once you start, you're more likely to keep going.

Let's say your goal is to get in shape. Your first baby step isn't running a 5K or signing up for a gym membership. It's putting on your sneakers. That's it. Once you've done that, your next step might be walking to the end of your driveway. Then around the block. Then maybe a full workout.

The key is to make the first step so ridiculously easy that you can't say no. Because once you've started, momentum takes over—and that's where the magic happens.

The Art of Lowering the Bar

Let's talk about your standards for a second. If you're anything like me, you probably have a tendency to set the bar way too high. *"I'm going to drink a gallon of water every day, meditate for 30 minutes, and write 2,000 words before breakfast!"* Sound familiar?

Here's the problem: When you set the bar too high, you're setting yourself up for failure. And when you fail, you're more likely to give up entirely.

So, instead of aiming for the stars right out of the gate, start by aiming for the curb. Set the bar so low that you can trip over it. Because guess what? Progress is progress, no matter how small. And once you've cleared that first hurdle, you can raise the bar little by little.

Baby Steps in Action

Still not convinced? Let's look at some real-life examples of baby steps in action:

1. **Goal: Eat Healthier**
   - Baby Step: Add one vegetable to your dinner tonight. (Yes, ketchup counts if you're desperate.)
2. **Goal: Be More Organized**
   - Baby Step: Spend five minutes tidying up your desk. Not the whole house—just your desk.
3. **Goal: Exercise More**
   - Baby Step: Do one push-up. Just one. If you feel ambitious, maybe two.
4. **Goal: Save Money**
   - Baby Step: Transfer $5 into your savings account. Congratulations, you're officially a financial genius.

Notice a pattern? Each of these steps is so small that they almost seem silly. But that's the point. Small steps build confidence, and confidence builds momentum.

Dealing with the "But It's Not Enough" Monster

At this point, you might be thinking, *"Okay, but one push-up isn't going to get me in shape. And $5 isn't going to make me a millionaire. What's the point?"*

First of all, calm down, Kevin. Second, let me remind you that progress isn't about making giant leaps—it's about taking consistent steps in the right direction.

Think about it: A single drop of water doesn't seem like much, but over time, enough drops can fill a bucket. The same goes for your goals. Each baby step might not seem like much on its own, but when you string them together, they add up to something incredible.

What to Do When You Trip

Let's be real: Even with the best intentions, you're going to trip over your own metaphorical shoelaces at some point. Maybe you'll skip a step, take a detour, or fall flat on your face. And that's okay.

The important thing is not to let one misstep derail your progress. Instead of beating yourself up, treat it as a learning opportunity. Ask yourself: *What went wrong? What can I do differently next time?* Then get back on track and keep moving forward.

Remember: Progress isn't linear. It's more like a wobbly zigzag with occasional faceplants. But as long as you're moving in the right direction, you're winning.

The Power of Accountability

Here's a pro tip: Baby steps are even more effective when you have someone to hold you accountable. Whether it's a friend, a partner, or a random stranger on the internet, having someone to check in with can make a huge difference.

Your accountability buddy doesn't have to be a drill sergeant (unless you're into that sort of thing). They just need to be someone who will cheer you on, encourage you when you're struggling, and maybe give you a gentle nudge when you're tempted to quit.

Procrastination thrives in isolation. Accountability thrives in community. So, if you've been trying to go it alone, now's the time to recruit some reinforcements.

Pause for Reflection:

Patience is often misunderstood as the act of simply waiting for something to happen. But in truth, patience is a force of nature—it's an active choice that requires presence, trust, and a willingness to let things unfold in their own time. Think about the times when impatience crept in—when you were rushing to reach a destination or fix a situation, only to find that your haste led to mistakes or frustration. Reflect for a moment on a time when you were patient—truly patient—when you allowed life to unfold naturally without trying to force the outcome. How did it feel? How did it affect the result? In this chapter, we'll explore how patience isn't about inaction; it's about learning to navigate life's challenges with calm and grace. Take a deep breath and ask yourself: What can I practice patience with today?

Baby Steps and the Snowball Effect

Let's get a little metaphorical here: Baby steps are like rolling a snowball down a hill. At first, it's small and unimpressive—just a handful of snow, really. But as it rolls, it picks up more snow, gaining size, speed, and momentum until suddenly you've got an unstoppable force of nature barreling downhill.

That's the power of small actions. Each one builds on the last, creating a chain reaction that leads to massive change over time. But here's the catch: You have to keep the snowball moving. Even if it's just one tiny push a day, consistency is what turns a little snowball into an avalanche of progress.

When Progress Feels Slow

Now, let's address the elephant in the room: Progress feels slow because it *is* slow. And that can be maddening when you're used to instant gratification. (Thanks, Amazon Prime.)

But here's the thing: Slow progress is still progress. Think of it like planting a garden. You don't plant seeds and expect a full-blown tomato plant the next day. You water them, tend to them, and give them time to grow. The same goes for your goals.

So, instead of focusing on how far you still must go, take a moment to appreciate how far you've already come. Celebrate the small wins, even if they feel insignificant. Because every tiny step forward is proof that you're moving in the right direction.

The Magic of Habit Stacking

Let's introduce a little hack to make baby steps even more effective: habit stacking. This is where you take a habit you already do regularly and "stack" a new habit on top of it.

For example:

- Every time you brush your teeth, spend one minute stretching.
- Every time you make your morning coffee, write down one thing you're grateful for.
- Every time you sit down to watch TV, do 10 squats during the commercial break (or hit "skip intro" and use that time wisely).

Habit stacking works because it ties your new action to something you're already doing, making it easier to remember and harder to ignore. Plus, it's a sneaky way to build momentum without feeling like you're adding more to your plate.

Don't Compare Your Snowball to Someone Else's Avalanche

Here's a quick reminder: Your journey is *yours*. Not your best friend's, not your coworker's, not that fitness influencer with a six-pack and a Pinterest-perfect morning routine.

It's easy to fall into the trap of comparison, especially when social media makes everyone else's life look like a highlight reel. But remember: You're only seeing the finished product, not the messy, awkward baby steps it took to get there.

So, instead of comparing your progress to someone else's, focus on staying in your own lane. Celebrate your wins, no matter how small, and trust that your snowball will grow at its own pace.

Baby Steps Aren't Sexy (But They're Effective)

Let's be honest: Baby steps aren't glamorous. Nobody's going to give you a standing ovation for putting on your sneakers or drinking a glass of water. But you know what is sexy? Results.

Results come from consistency, and consistency comes from baby steps. So, while everyone else is burning out trying to do too much too fast, you're quietly building a foundation for success that lasts.

Think of yourself as the tortoise in the tortoise-and-hare story. Sure, the hare gets all the attention at first, but who wins in the end? That's right—you, the slow and steady tortoise, with your unshakable commitment to progress.

Building a Baby Step Routine

Okay, let's get practical. Here's how to create a daily routine that revolves around baby steps:

1. **Start Small**: Pick one or two tiny actions to focus on each day. (Remember: stupidly small is the goal.)

2. **Schedule It**: Decide when and where you'll do these actions. Tie them to an existing habit or routine to make them easier to remember.

3. **Track Your Progress**: Use a journal, app, or even a sticky note to keep track of your wins. Seeing your progress in black and white is incredibly motivating.

4. **Adjust as Needed**: If something isn't working, tweak it. Baby steps are flexible, not rigid.

Your routine doesn't have to be perfect—it just must be consistent. Consistency is key to making these efforts as part of your daily routines. Start with making them part of your routine every day by writing them down, creating a checklist. Remember, even a 50% success rate is better than doing nothing at all.

Baby Steps and Self-Compassion

Let's talk about the most important part of this whole process: being kind to yourself.

Change is hard. You're going to mess up. You're going to have days when you feel like giving up. And that's okay. The key is to treat yourself with the same compassion and understanding you'd offer a friend who's struggling.

Instead of beating yourself up for falling short, remind yourself that progress is messy and non-linear. Celebrate the effort, not just the outcome. And when in doubt, ask yourself, *"What would I say to someone I care about in this situation?"* Then say that to yourself.

Homework Time

Before we wrap up this chapter, let's put all this baby step wisdom into action. Here's your homework:

1. **Pick a Goal**: Choose one small, specific goal you want to work on this week.
2. **Identify Your First Baby Step**: What's the tiniest possible action you can take to move toward that goal? Write it down.
3. **Set a Trigger**: Find a way to tie your baby step to an existing habit or routine (hello, habit stacking!).

4. **Track Your Wins**: Create a simple way to track your progress—whether it's a checkmark on a calendar or a gold star sticker (yes, adults can use stickers).

Optional Homework Time:

1. **Patience in Action:** Think of something in your life that you're currently impatient about—whether it's a goal, a situation, or even a relationship. For the next week, commit to being more patient with it. When impatience arises, pause, breathe, and remind yourself that good things take time. Write down your feelings as you practice patience, and reflect on how it changes your perspective.

2. **Slow Down Challenge:** Choose an activity that you usually rush through—like eating, driving, or completing a task at work—and slow it down. Approach it with full awareness and attention. Notice the details you usually overlook when you're rushing. Write down how this change in pace affects your experience. You might be surprised by the clarity that comes from slowing down.

3. **Patience with Yourself:** We often show more patience to others than we do to ourselves. This week, identify a time when you've been hard on yourself for not achieving something quickly enough. Practice showing yourself the same kindness and patience you would show a friend. Write about your experience and how it feels to give yourself permission to take your time.

End of Chapter Exercises:

1. **Patience Reflection Journal:** At the end of each day for the next week, take a moment to reflect on any moments where you practiced patience. Write about what you learned from these moments and how they made you feel. Over time, you'll

begin to see how patience changes your experience of life, helping you navigate challenges with more ease.

2. **The One-Thing Practice:** Pick one area in your life where impatience tends to show up. It could be a project, a relationship, or a long-term goal. Each day, commit to doing just one thing toward that goal—but with patience. Whether it's taking small steps, allowing things to unfold naturally, or simply letting go of the need to control everything, track your progress and reflect on how patience affects the outcome.

3. **Patience Visualization:** Spend 5-10 minutes visualizing yourself in a challenging situation that usually triggers impatience. See yourself responding with calm, patience, and acceptance. Visualize the outcome unfolding naturally, without force. This mental exercise will train your mind to handle impatience with grace when the real situation arises.

Key Takeaways:

- **Patience Is a Choice, Not a Passive Act:** True patience doesn't mean inaction. It's about choosing to trust the process, to give things time, and to stay present in the moment, rather than rushing toward a destination.

- **Haste Often Leads to Mistakes:** When you rush through life, you miss important details, make mistakes, and create unnecessary stress. Slowing down and practicing patience allows you to make better decisions and avoid unnecessary frustration.

- **Patience Builds Resilience:** When you practice patience, you build the mental and emotional strength to handle life's challenges without becoming overwhelmed. Patience teaches you to endure, persevere, and trust that everything will unfold as it should.

- **Patience Is About Trust:** At its core, patience is about trusting the process of life. Trusting that things will unfold in their own time and that you don't need to rush to make them happen.

- **Patience Doesn't Mean Waiting Idle:** Patience is active. It's about making progress while also accepting that things take time. It's about finding peace in the journey, not just the destination.

Cheat Sheets & Recaps:

- **Patience Is Active:** Patience is not about waiting passively—it's about choosing to be present and trusting that things will unfold at the right time.

- **Slowing Down Leads to Clarity:** When you slow down, you allow yourself to see things clearly. Patience helps you avoid unnecessary mistakes and makes space for better decision-making.

- **Patience Is Practice:** You don't build patience overnight. It's something that you cultivate through small, conscious choices. The more you practice, the more natural it becomes.

- **Trust the Process:** The key to patience is trust. Trust that life is unfolding exactly as it should, and that rushing won't change that. Embrace the journey and let go of the need for control.

- **The Power of Small Steps:** When you practice patience, you're able to take small, deliberate steps toward your goal without feeling overwhelmed. Each small step, taken with patience, leads to big progress over time.

Kenism: *"The rake strikes you, but it is not the rake you fear—it is the consequence of the strike. But in that moment, there is an opportunity to look within. What is it that makes us fear the rake? It is not the rake itself, but our lack of preparation. The more you prepare to sidestep the rakes of life, the faster you are to respond to rakes in the future. Then you become more prepared to face life's challenges, and the less we will fear them. So, the next time fear rises, step toward it, not away from it. Know that with every challenge, there is a lesson waiting to be learned. Fear is just a signal—it is telling you where your growth lies."*

Final Thoughts

Baby steps might not be flashy or exciting, but they're the foundation of real, lasting change. They're how you build momentum, overcome self-doubt, and create a life that feels meaningful and fulfilling.

So, don't underestimate the power of small actions. Every tiny step you take is a victory, a sign that you're moving in the right direction. And if you keep putting one foot in front of the other, there's no limit to how far you can go.

Now, take a deep breath, give yourself a well-deserved pat on the back, and get ready for Chapter 4. The journey continues, and you're doing better than you think.

TL;DR: Patience is more than just waiting—it's a conscious choice to trust the process and allow things to unfold naturally. Rushing through life only leads to mistakes and frustration, but when you practice patience, you build resilience, clarity, and peace. In this chapter, we learned how to slow down, be present, and embrace the journey with patience. The key to navigating life's challenges is not speed, but trusting that everything will happen in its own time.

Notes:

Chapter 4: How to Fail Like a Pro

Kenism: *"You cannot avoid the rakes in life. You will step on them, and they will strike you—sometimes with great force. The question is not about avoiding the strike, but about embracing the lessons that come with it. You see, the rake is not a punishment; it is an invitation. An invitation to wake up and understand that life's challenges are not obstacles but invitations for transformation. When you embrace the rake, you are embracing the possibility of growth and awareness that lies just beyond the strike."*

Ah, failure. That cringe-worthy, stomach-turning, curl-up-in-a-ball-and-pretend-it-didn't-happen word. If you're human—and I'm assuming you are—you've experienced failure. Maybe it was a big, public faceplant, or maybe it was a private "oops" moment that only you know about. Either way, failure is part of the package deal called life.

The problem is, most of us have been taught to see failure as the enemy. We're told to avoid it at all costs, to sweep it under the rug, to slap a filter on it and pretend it never happened. But here's the truth: Failure isn't the enemy. It's a messy, misunderstood, occasionally embarrassing friend who shows up uninvited but always leaves you with something valuable.

So, in this chapter, we're going to reframe failure. We're going to strip away the shame and learn how to fail like a pro. Because the truth is, failure isn't just inevitable, it's essential. And if you can learn to embrace it, you'll be unstoppable.

Why Failure Feels So Terrible

Let's start with the obvious: Failure sucks. It feels bad. It's uncomfortable, awkward, and sometimes downright humiliating. But why?

Blame it on your brain. Your brain is wired to avoid pain, both physical and emotional. Back in the caveman days, avoiding pain meant not getting eaten by a saber-toothed tiger. These days, it means not getting metaphorically eaten by judgment, criticism, or the crushing weight of your own expectations.

Failure triggers your brain's fight-or-flight response. It tells you, *"This is dangerous! Run away! Hide under a blanket and pretend you're not home!"* And while that instinct might have kept you alive in prehistoric times, it's not exactly helpful when you're trying to learn, grow, and achieve your goals.

The Truth About Failure

Here's the truth nobody tells you: Failure isn't a reflection of your worth. It's not a character flaw or a moral failing. It's just feedback.

Think of failure like a GPS recalculating your route. When you make a wrong turn, the GPS doesn't scream, *"You're a terrible driver and you'll never make it to your destination!"* It calmly says, *"Recalculating,"* and gives you a new direction.

That's what failure does. It shows you what didn't work so you can adjust your approach and try again. It's not personal; it's just part of the process.

Famous Failures (AKA, You're in Good Company)

Still not convinced? Let's look at some people who failed spectacularly before finding success:

- **Thomas Edison**: Failed over 10,000 times before inventing the lightbulb. When asked about his failures, he said, *"I have not failed. I've just found 10,000 ways that won't work."*
- **J.K. Rowling**: Rejected by 12 publishers before Harry Potter became a global phenomenon. Imagine being one of those publishers now.
- **Oprah Winfrey**: Fired from her first TV job because she was "unfit for television." Let that sink in for a second.
- **Michael Jordan**: Cut from his high school basketball team. He famously said, *"I've missed more than 9,000 shots in my career. I've lost almost 300 games. On 26 occasions, I've been trusted to take the game-winning shot and missed. I've failed over and over and over again in my life. And that is why I succeed."*

See? Failure isn't just normal—it's a prerequisite for greatness.

How to Fail Like a Pro

Alright, let's get practical. How do you actually fail in a way that helps you grow instead of crushing your soul?

1. Reframe the Narrative

Stop thinking of failure as the end of the road and start seeing it as a stepping stone. Every failure is a chance to learn, improve, and get closer to your goal. Instead of saying, *"I failed,"* try saying, *"I learned."*

2. Detach Your Ego

One of the reasons failure hurts so much is because we take it personally. We see it as a reflection of who we are instead of what we did. Newsflash: You are not your failures. They're just things that happened.

3. Find the Lesson

Every failure has something to teach you, even if it's just, *"Don't do that again."* Take a moment to reflect on what went wrong, what you could have done differently, and what you'll do next time.

4. Embrace the Awkwardness

Failure is awkward, and that's okay. Lean into it. Laugh about it. Share your story with a friend who won't judge you (or who has their own embarrassing stories to share).

5. Keep Going

The only way to truly fail is to give up. And why would you give up, is it fear, laziness, inconvenience? Think through your reasons for wanting to give up and remind yourself that you can think these things, but you must not give into them. Stand up and make the effort to do thins differently. And, as long as you're still trying, you're still in the game playing with everyone else. Remember: Progress isn't linear. It's a wobbly, zigzagging, occasionally faceplant-filled journey, and that's what makes it worth it.

Turning Failure into Fuel

Here's the cool thing about failure: It can be a powerful motivator. We all fail at life, sometimes over and over again, and that's part of life for all of us. When you fail, you have two choices: You can let it defeat you, or you can use it as fuel to prove yourself wrong (or prove your haters wrong, if that's more your style).

The next time you fail, channel your inner Beyoncé. Remember how she fell during a concert and got back up like nothing happened? Be like Beyoncé. Get back up, shake it off, and keep going like the unstoppable badass you are.

Homework Time

Before we wrap up this chapter, let's put some of these ideas into action. Here's your homework:

1. **Reframe a Recent Failure**: Think of a time you failed recently. Write down what happened, what you learned, and how you can use that experience to grow.

2. **Celebrate a Failure**: Yes, you read that right. Pick a failure that taught you something valuable and celebrate it. Treat yourself to a cupcake, do a little victory dance, or just give yourself a mental high five.

3. **Make a Failure Plan**: Identify one area where you're afraid to fail and come up with a plan for how you'll handle it if things don't go as expected.

Pause for Reflection:

You've made it through the first half of the book, and now we're diving into the glorious art of failure. If you're thinking, "Wait, I'm supposed to embrace failing?" you're in the right place. Take a moment to consider this: What have you failed at recently? And more importantly, what did that failure teach you? Was it a lesson about patience? Perseverance? The importance of humility (and maybe not trying to climb a mountain in flip-flops)? In this chapter, we're going to flip the script on failure—transforming it from something you run from to something you sprint toward, face-first and with your eyes wide open.

The Sixth Step: Laugh at Your Failures

Laughter might not solve all your problems, but it can make them a whole lot easier to bear. When you fail, your first instinct might be to wallow in shame or frustration. Instead, try finding the humor in the situation.

Did you accidentally send an email to your entire company instead of just your boss? Hilarious. Did you trip on the treadmill and fall face-first in front of a gym full of people? Iconic. These moments might feel mortifying in the moment, but in the grand scheme of things, they're just funny stories you'll tell later.

Laughter takes the sting out of failure. It reminds you that life doesn't have to be so serious, and neither do you. So, the next time you fail, channel your inner stand-up comedian and find the punchline.

The Seventh Step: Share Your Failures

This one might sound weird, but hear me out: Sharing your failures can be incredibly liberating.

Think about how often do you feel like you're the only one who's messing up, while everyone else has their life perfectly together? Spoiler alert: They don't. Everyone is failing in their own unique, ridiculous way, they're just not talking about it.

When you share your failures, you give others permission to do the same. You create a space where people can be honest, vulnerable, and human. Plus, you might even inspire someone else to keep going despite their own setbacks.

So, don't be afraid to share your failures. Post about them, laugh about them, or bring them up at dinner parties. (Trust me, "That time I accidentally flooded my apartment" makes for a way better story than "Everything is perfect, and I've never struggled.")

The Eighth Step: Redefine Success

Let's redefine what success means. For most of us, success is this abstract, unattainable thing—a combination of wealth, power, happiness, and the ability to eat tacos without spilling salsa on your shirt.

But here's the problem: When success feels unattainable, failure feels inevitable. That's why it's so important to redefine success in a way that feels achievable, meaningful, and aligned with your values.

Ask yourself: What does success look like for *me*? Maybe it's being a little kinder to yourself. Maybe it's taking one small step toward your goals every day. Maybe it's just surviving another Monday without losing your mind. Whatever it is, make it personal, specific, and realistic.

When you redefine success, failure stops feeling like a personal attack and starts feeling like a natural part of the journey.

Failure as a Feedback Loop

Here's a game-changing perspective: Failure isn't an endpoint; it's a feedback loop. It's like a video game where every time you lose a life, you learn a little more about how to beat the boss.

Instead of seeing failure as a reason to quit, see it as a data point. What worked? What didn't? What can you do differently next time?

The key is to approach failure with curiosity instead of judgment. Treat it like an experiment. Try something, see what happens, and adjust accordingly. The more you experiment, the more you learn— and the closer you get to success.

The Fear of What Others Think

Let's address the elephant in the room: One of the biggest reasons we fear failure is because we're worried about what other people will think.

Will they judge you? Maybe. Will they gossip about you? Possibly. Will they forget all about it in a week because they're too busy worrying about their own lives? Absolutely.

Here's the truth: Most people are too wrapped up in their own drama to care about your failures. And the ones who *do* care? They're probably just projecting their own insecurities onto you. So, stop letting the opinions of others dictate your actions.

You're not living your life for an audience. You're living it for yourself. And if you fail along the way, that's just part of the show.

How to Bounce Back from Failure

Bouncing back from failure isn't about pretending it didn't happen. It's about acknowledging it, learning from it, and moving forward. Here's a step-by-step guide:

1. **Feel the Feelings**: It's okay to feel disappointed, frustrated, or even a little embarrassed. Allow yourself to process those emotions without judgment.

2. **Reflect on the Experience**: Take some time to think about what went wrong and why. Was it a lack of preparation? Bad timing? Something completely out of your control?

3. **Identify the Lesson**: What can you learn from this failure? How can you use that knowledge to improve next time?

4. **Make a Plan**: Decide what your next steps will be. Be specific and actionable.

5. **Move On**: Once you've done the work, let it go. Don't dwell on the failure—focus on the future.

Homework Time

Before we move on to the next chapter, let's turn all this talk about failure into action. Here's your homework:

1. **Embrace a Failure**: Think of a time you failed recently. Instead of beating yourself up, write down three things you learned from the experience.

2. **Redefine Success**: Take a few minutes to write down what success looks like for you. Make it personal, realistic, and aligned with your values.

3. **Plan for Your Next Failure**: Choose one area where you want to take a risk, and make a plan for how you'll handle it if things don't go as expected.

4. **Share Your Story**: Tell a trusted friend, family member, or even a stranger about a time you failed and what you learned from it.

Homework Time:

1. **Fail Forward:** Think of one recent failure you've experienced. Write it down. No, you're not allowed to ignore this—it's your homework! Now, for each failure, write down what it taught you. And no, the lesson isn't always about how to avoid failure next time; it's also about how to embrace it. For example, maybe you tried something new, and it didn't go as planned. Did you learn something new about yourself or the process?

2. **Embrace Imperfection:** Pick a task that you've been putting off because you're trying to make it perfect. It's time to let go of that perfectionist grip. Do it this week, but don't aim for perfection. Aim for progress. And remember, the only mistake you can make is not starting at all.

3. **Tell Your Failure Story:** Find a friend, an AI you trust and use on a regular basis, or family member and share a story of a failure that you've overcome. Bonus points if you can laugh about it. The purpose of this exercise is to normalize failure

and not give it more power than it deserves. Remember to talk through the failure in a positive learning manner. Today so many people are afraid to admit failures. But we all need to see that sharing your failure with others helps others as well. Why? Because not only will you learn from them, they will too.

End of Chapter Exercises:

1. **Failure Reflection Journal:** Spend 10 minutes each day writing in a failure journal. Not every entry needs to be deep or profound. Write down moments where things didn't go as planned, and how you handled them. The goal here is to build a habit of seeing failure as a normal part of life.

2. **Failure Action Plan:** Next time you face a failure, create a simple action plan. This could be three steps on how you will address the failure and what small changes you can make moving forward. Remember: your plan isn't about eradicating failure; it's about learning from it.

3. **Failure Gratitude List:** Make a list of all the things you've learned from your biggest failures. Include things like patience, perseverance, and what you would do differently next time. These lists might make you chuckle when you realize how far you've come since your last "disaster."

Key Takeaways:

- **Failure is Not the Enemy:** It's the teacher that shows you the way forward. Failure provides critical lessons—so learn from it instead of avoiding it.

- **Small Wins Lead to Big Successes:** Reframe failure as a series of small setbacks that are essential to progress. Every failure is a stepping stone.

- **Perfection Is the Killer of Progress:** Don't get trapped in the illusion of perfection. Move forward with what you have and improve along the way.

- **Embrace the Process:** Realize that mistakes will happen; it's what you do afterward that matters. Accept the learning process, and be kinder to yourself when things go wrong.

- **Share Your Failures:** Talking about your failures doesn't make you weak; it normalizes them. The more you share, the less power they have over you.

Cheat Sheets & Recaps:

- **Mistake-Resilience:** Mistakes aren't a sign of failure; they're part of the learning process. Develop resilience by embracing mistakes, rather than avoiding them. The quicker you make peace with your mistakes, the quicker you can turn them into valuable lessons.

- **Failures Aren't Permanent:** One failure doesn't define you. It's just a moment in time. Keep moving forward, and soon enough, the sting will fade, and you'll see the lesson more clearly.

- **Perfectionism is an Illusion:** Perfection keeps you stuck. Aim for progress over perfection every time. You have to realize that the Good Enough Principile exists for a reason. If it's 95% close to perfect, then it's good enough!

- **Shift Your Mindset:** Don't view setbacks as something to fear. Instead, look at them as opportunities to build resilience, learn, and grow.

- **Laugh at Your Failures:** Remember, you're human. Laugh at your failures as you would laugh at a funny moment in a sitcom. They're part of the ride, not the destination.

Kenism: *"When you stop fighting the rake, when you stop trying to avoid it, you begin to see it for what it truly is: a teacher. Life's challenges are not here to break you; they are here to show you who you are. So, every time you step on the rake, pause and ask yourself: What is this moment teaching me? How can I grow from this pain? The true power lies not in avoiding life's difficulties, but in learning to dance with them—turning every rake into a moment of clarity and growth."*

Final Thoughts

Failure isn't the enemy—it's the teacher. It's the stepping stone that helps you grow, the recalibration that sets you on the right path, and sometimes, the hilarious story you'll laugh about later.

Failure isn't fun, but it's also not the end of the world. It's a stepping stone, a learning opportunity, and sometimes even a blessing in disguise. If you can learn to fail like a pro, you'll be unstoppable.

So, the next time you fall flat on your face, remember this: You're not failing—you're growing. And if you keep getting back up, there's no limit to what you can achieve.

Now, take a deep breath, dust yourself off, and get ready for the next chapter. Because failure isn't the end—it's just the beginning.

If you can learn to embrace failure, you'll unlock a level of resilience, creativity, and grit that most people only dream of. So, go ahead—fail big, fail often, and fail like a pro. Because every time you fail, you're one step closer to success.

Now, take a deep breath, give yourself a high five (or a fist bump if you're feeling fancy), and get ready for Chapter 5. The journey continues, and you're doing better than you think.

TL;DR: Failure is not a bad thing—it's a powerful tool for growth. If you keep avoiding failure, you'll never learn anything. The key is to stop fearing it and start embracing it. Don't strive for perfection, but progress. Every failure is just a lesson in disguise. Write down your failures, learn from them, and celebrate the small wins. Progress, not perfection!

Chapter 5: Stop Chasing Motivation—Build Momentum Instead

Chapter 5: The Power of Presence

Kenism: *"Presence is the antidote to the chaos of life. We are constantly rushing through our days, lost in thoughts of the future or regrets about the past. But presence—being fully in the moment—changes everything. It allows you to see the rake before it strikes, to feel the world around you with clarity and purpose. Presence is the art of being aware in real time. It's not about preparing for the future, but being alert in the now, where the rakes lie waiting to teach you."*

Ah, motivation—the mythical creature of the self-help world. Everyone talks about it like it's the key to unlocking your best life, but let's be real: Motivation is about as reliable as a drunk weather forecaster. Some days, it shows up, bright and enthusiastic, promising blue skies and productivity. Other days, it ghosts you completely, leaving you stuck in sweatpants binge-watching Netflix and eating cereal out of the box.

Here's the cold, hard truth: Motivation is overrated. It's fleeting, unpredictable, and—brace yourself—it's not even necessary. That's right. You don't need motivation to get things done. What you need is *momentum*.

In this chapter, we're going to break up with motivation and learn how to build momentum instead. Because while motivation is great when it shows up, momentum is what keeps you moving forward when it doesn't.

Why Motivation Fails You

Let's start by unpacking why motivation doesn't work. It's not because you're lazy, uncommitted, or secretly allergic to effort (though that's a great excuse if you're looking for one). It's because motivation is rooted in emotion.

Motivation relies on you *feeling* like doing something. And while emotions can be powerful, they're also fickle. One minute you're fired up to start a new project, and the next, you're questioning every life choice that led you to this moment.

Motivation is a fair-weather friend. It shows up when things are easy and exciting but vanishes the second things get hard. Momentum, on the other hand, doesn't care how you feel. It's the workhorse of progress, steady and dependable, carrying you forward even on the days when you'd rather do literally anything else.

The Science of Momentum

Momentum isn't just a motivational buzzword—it's science. In physics, momentum is the product of mass and velocity. In plain English, that means it's easier to keep something moving once it's already in motion.

The same principle applies to your life. When you're stuck at a standstill, everything feels hard. But once you take that first step, the next one feels a little easier, and the one after that even easier. Momentum builds on itself, creating a snowball effect that turns small actions into big results.

The best part? You don't need to feel motivated to start building momentum. All you need is to take one tiny, imperfect action.

How to Build Momentum from Scratch

So, how do you build momentum when you're starting at zero? Simple: You lower the bar.

No, not that kind of bar. I'm talking about setting the bar so low that it's impossible to fail. The goal isn't to accomplish something monumental, it's to take one tiny step that gets you moving.

Here's how:

1. **Start Small**
    - Stupidly small. Like, so small that it feels almost ridiculous. If your goal is to start working out, don't aim for a full hour at the gym. Start with putting on your sneakers. That's it.

2. **Celebrate Every Win**
    - Each small action you take is a victory, and victories deserve to be celebrated. High-five yourself, do a little dance, or treat yourself to something you love.

3. **Focus on Consistency, Not Intensity**
    - Momentum is about showing up, not showing off. A five-minute walk every day is more effective than a two-hour workout once a month.

4. **Use the Two-Minute Rule**
    - Commit to doing something for just two minutes. Once you start, you'll often find it easier to keep going. And if not, hey, you still did two minutes—win!

Momentum in Action

Let's look at some real-life examples of how momentum works:

Example 1: The "I'll Just" Trick

Ever notice how saying "I'll just" makes things feel less overwhelming?

- *"I'll just write one sentence."*
- *"I'll just clean one corner of the room."*
- *"I'll just make one phone call."*

Nine times out of ten, you'll end up doing more than you planned. But even if you don't, you've still taken a step forward—and that's momentum.

Example 2: The Domino Effect

Momentum has a way of spreading to other areas of your life. For example, deciding to drink a glass of water in the morning might lead to making a healthier breakfast choice, which might lead to feeling more energized, which might lead to tackling that project you've been avoiding.

Small actions create ripples, and those ripples add up to big waves.

Breaking Through the "Motivation Dip"

Even with momentum on your side, you're going to hit a motivation dip—a moment (or several) when you feel like giving up. This is normal. It's also where most people quit.

Here's how to power through:

1. **Remember Your "Why"**
    - Why did you start this journey in the first place? Write it down and keep it somewhere visible. Your "why" is your anchor when things get tough.

2. **Lower the Bar Again**
    - If you're struggling, go back to basics. What's the smallest possible step you can take to keep moving forward?
3. **Use Accountability**
    - Tell someone about your goals and ask them to check in on you. Knowing someone else is rooting for you can be a powerful motivator.
4. **Forgive Yourself**
    - Missed a day? Fell off track? No big deal. Momentum isn't about being perfect—it's about getting back up and keeping the ball rolling.

Momentum vs. Motivation: A Love Story

Think of motivation and momentum as two very different relationships. Motivation is the passionate, whirlwind romance that burns hot and fizzles fast. Momentum is the steady, reliable partner who's always there for you, even on your worst days.

Sure, motivation might sweep you off your feet every now and then, but momentum is the one you want to build a life with. So, stop chasing motivation and start committing to momentum.

Homework Time

Let's put this momentum-building magic into action. Here's your homework for this chapter:

1. **Pick One Tiny Action**: Choose one ridiculously small step you can take today to move closer to your goal. Write it down.

2. **Celebrate the Win**: After you take that action, celebrate it in some way, big or small.
3. **Start a Momentum Journal**: Keep track of the small steps you take each day. Seeing your progress in black and white is a great way to stay motivated.
4. **Find Your "Why"**: Write down why this goal matters to you and keep it somewhere visible.

Extra Thoughts

Motivation might be flashy and exciting, but momentum is what gets the job done. It's the quiet, persistent force that turns small actions into big changes. And the best part? You don't have to wait for motivation to strike—you can start building momentum right now.

So, take that first tiny step, no matter how small. Keep the ball rolling, even when it feels slow. And remember: Progress isn't about how fast you go, it's about showing up, day after day, and trusting that every step forward matters.

Pause for Reflection:

Here we are, moving through this journey, and what do we find? The biggest obstacle often isn't failure but simply *being present*. In the whirlwind of our fast-paced lives, we lose sight of the moment right in front of us. The rakes keep appearing in the background, waiting to trip us up, but how often do we notice them? What if the secret to not stepping on the rake is not being faster, but *slowing down* enough to see it clearly? Pause for a moment and think—how often do you find yourself rushing through life, missing the cues, the lessons, the opportunities that are right in front of you? In this chapter, we dive into the power of presence, learning how to step with awareness and navigate life with purpose.

The Power of Ritual: Momentum's Secret Weapon

Here's a little-known fact about momentum: It loves rituals. Rituals are like the cozy sweatpants of productivity—they make everything more comfortable and easier to stick with.

What's a ritual, you ask? It's just a fancy way of saying *a consistent routine that signals to your brain it's time to get moving.* Rituals create a mental shortcut that eliminates the "Should I? Shouldn't I?" debate.

For example:

- Every morning, you make coffee, sit down at your desk, and write for 15 minutes. That's a ritual.
- Before every workout, you lace up your sneakers and listen to your "pump-up" playlist. Ritual.
- Before bed, you write down three wins from your day. You guessed it: ritual.

Rituals don't have to be elaborate. In fact, the simpler, the better. The key is consistency. The more you repeat the ritual, the more automatic it becomes, and the less effort it takes to get started.

Momentum Killers: Beware the Saboteurs

While we're on a roll, let's talk about the things that kill momentum faster than a poorly timed sneeze during a karaoke performance. Watch for these saboteurs:

1. Overthinking

Overthinking is momentum's arch-nemesis. It convinces you to analyze every detail, weigh every option, and procrastinate until the opportunity passes.

The solution? Adopt a "done is better than perfect" mindset. Take action, even if it's messy or imperfect. You can always adjust later.

2. Comparison

Nothing slows you down like looking at someone else's highlight reel and thinking, *"Why even bother?"* Remember: Your journey is unique. Stop comparing your chapter one to someone else's chapter 20.

3. Distractions

Let's face it: We live in a world designed to distract you. Social media, Netflix, your neighbor's drama—it's all vying for your attention.

Combat distractions by setting boundaries. Turn off notifications, create a dedicated workspace, and give yourself permission to focus.

The "Momentum Boosters" Toolkit

Now that you know what to avoid, let's talk about how to supercharge your momentum. These simple boosters can help you stay on track, even when the going gets tough:

1. The Pomodoro Technique

Work for 25 minutes, then take a 5-minute break. Repeat. This technique helps you stay focused and avoid burnout while building momentum in bite-sized chunks.

2. Visual Progress Trackers

There's something satisfying about seeing your progress visually. Whether it's crossing off days on a calendar, filling in a habit tracker, or sticking gold stars on a chart, find a way to celebrate your wins.

3. Rewards

Give yourself something to look forward to when you hit a milestone. It can be an extravagant fancy coffee, a bubble bath, or watching your favorite show. Each of these can do the trick.

4. Stacking Wins

Start your day with an easy win. Make your bed, drink a glass of water, or tackle a small task. Each win builds momentum for the next.

The Psychology of "Showing Up"

Let's get nerdy for a second. Psychologists have found that the simple act of "showing up" is one of the most powerful predictors of success.

Why? Because showing up builds trust—not just with others, but with yourself. Every time you follow through on a commitment, you reinforce the belief that you're capable, reliable, and worthy of success.

Therefore, small actions matter so much. They're not just about moving closer to your goal; they're about building confidence and self-respect. And when you believe in yourself, momentum becomes unstoppable.

Momentum and Self-Compassion

Here's the thing about momentum: It's not a straight line. There are days when you crush it and days when you feel you're dragging yourself through wet cement. And that's okay.

The key is to approach yourself with compassion. Instead of beating yourself up for a "bad" day, remind yourself that progress is a marathon, not a sprint. Celebrate the fact that you're still in the race, even if you're moving slower than you'd like.

Momentum doesn't require perfection. It just requires persistence.

Real-Life Momentum Heroes

Need some inspiration? Let's talk about a few real-life examples of people who built incredible momentum, one small step at a time:

1. James Clear

Author of *Atomic Habits*, James Clear didn't become a bestselling author overnight. He started by writing one article a week on his blog. Over time, those articles gained traction, leading to book deals and a global audience.

2. Mel Robbins

Before she became a motivational powerhouse, Mel Robbins was struggling with anxiety and self-doubt. Her journey started with one small action: counting backward from five and taking action before her brain could talk her out of it.

3. You (Yes, You)

Think about a time when you achieved something you're proud of. Chances are, it didn't happen all at once. It happened because you took small, consistent steps that added up over time. That's momentum in action.

Homework Time

Before we wrap up this chapter, let's turn theory into practice. Here's your momentum-boosting homework:

1. **Create a Ritual**: Identify one small ritual you can add to your daily routine to kickstart momentum.
2. **Set a Visual Tracker**: Find a way to track your progress, whether it's a journal, an app, or a DIY chart.
3. **Tackle a Micro-Win**: Choose one tiny action you can take right now—yes, right now—and do it.
4. **Plan for Distractions**: Identify your biggest distractions and come up with a plan to minimize them.

Homework Time:

1. **Mindfulness Practice:** Spend five minutes each day focusing purely on your breath. Close your eyes, take slow, deep

breaths, and clear your mind of distractions. In those five minutes, simply *be present*. This exercise helps train your mind to stay in the moment, reducing the distractions that lead to stepping on metaphorical rakes.

2. **Slow Down and Observe:** Pick a daily activity you usually do on autopilot—like walking, eating, or driving. This week, do it with full presence. Engage all your senses. What do you see, hear, smell, and feel in those moments? Write down your experience afterward. You'll be surprised by how much you've been missing.

3. **Pause for Awareness:** Next time you feel overwhelmed or rushed, pause. Take a moment to stop, breathe, and center yourself. Reflect on what's happening around you. This simple act of pausing can help you prevent those "rake moments" before they happen.

End of Chapter Exercises:

1. **Presence Journal:** For the next seven days, keep a journal of moments when you practiced being present. Write down what you noticed, how it felt, and what impact it had on your day. The goal is to make presence a regular practice, not just something you do when you feel like it.

2. **Body Scan Exercise:** Every evening, take five minutes to do a body scan. Start from your toes and work your way up, noticing any tension, discomfort, or areas of ease. This exercise grounds you in the present moment and brings awareness to where you may be holding stress.

3. **One-Minute Pause:** Throughout your day, set a timer for one minute. When it rings, stop whatever you're doing and just *be*. Close your eyes, breathe deeply, and simply exist in the moment. In that minute, notice the clarity that arises when you focus only on being, not doing.

Key Takeaways:

- **Being Present Is Power:** The more present you are in the moment, the less likely you are to miss the cues life is giving you. Being aware of what's around you helps you avoid unnecessary pain and frustration.

- **Finding Clarity Through Slowing Down: Life's speed often causes us to make unintentional mistakes.** We can better predict and decide when we slow down.

- **Mindfulness Can Be Practiced Anywhere:** You don't need to retreat to a mountaintop to be present. With small, mindful practices woven into your day, you can cultivate a life of awareness and focus.

- **Presence Eases Overwhelm:** When you're fully present, the chaos of life becomes more manageable. You stop feeling overwhelmed because your attention is anchored in the here and now, not scattered across past regrets or future anxieties.

Cheat Sheets & Recaps:

- **Presence:** The art of being aware in the moment, unburdened by distractions.

- **Mindfulness:** Allows you to center your attention and stop operating on autopilot.

- **Slowing Down:** The key to seeing the rakes before they strike. When you slow down, you create space for awareness and clarity.

- **The Pause:** A simple tool to regain composure and focus. Use it throughout the day to refresh your mind and stay grounded.

- **Being Instead of Doing:** Shift from a mindset of doing everything at once to simply being present with what you're doing.

Kenism: *"When you are truly present, there is no fear of the rake. You see it coming before it strikes. You move with purpose, not reaction. Life, in its chaos, does not need to be feared when you are grounded in the present moment. So, slow down. Breathe. And feel the earth beneath your feet. In this space, the rakes are no longer obstacles. They are simply part of the journey. The more present you are, the less likely you are to step on the rake, and when you do, you will laugh, learn, and continue walking forward with greater wisdom."*

Final Thoughts

Momentum isn't about doing everything at once. It's about doing something, then something else, then something else, until suddenly you've built a wave of progress that carries you forward.

So, stop chasing motivation. Stop waiting for the perfect moment. Take a deep breath, lower the bar, and take one small step. Then another. Then another.

You've got this, my friend. The journey is just beginning, and with momentum on your side, there's no limit to where you can go.

Now, take a moment to celebrate the fact that you just crushed another chapter. Give yourself a fist bump, a gold star, or a victory snack (I vote for snacks). And get ready for Chapter 6. The best is yet to come.

TL;DR: Presence is your superpower. By slowing down, practicing mindfulness, and staying in the moment, you can prevent the chaos that leads to stepping on rakes. The more you practice presence, the more you see the opportunities around you and avoid the pitfalls of distractions and overwhelm. It's time to stop rushing and start living mindfully.

Notes:

Chapter 6: When Life Hands You Lemons, Throw Them at a Wall

Kenism: "In life, we often seek grand victories, but true growth is found in the smallest of wins. *The rake that strikes you today is not the end, but a stepping stone to greater awareness. Every small victory—the moment you step around a rake, the day you face your fears—adds up. The challenge is not to wait for a large change but to honor the tiny shifts, the imperceptible moments where you choose to learn, to grow. Just like a tree grows from the smallest seed, you build your journey one small, deliberate step at a time.*"

Ah, life. That unpredictable rollercoaster of highs, lows, and the occasional loop-de-loop that leaves you questioning everything, including why you even got on in the first place. At some point—or more likely, at many points—life is going to hand you lemons. And not the nice, fresh kind you'd use for a refreshing summer drink. No, we're talking about the kind that are bruised, sour, and aimed squarely at your head.

So, what do you do when life throws those metaphorical lemons your way? Do you grin and bear it? Make lemonade? Nah. Let's get real: sometimes you just need to chuck those suckers at a wall and scream into the void.

But after the initial tantrum (which is totally valid, by the way), it's time to regroup, refocus, and figure out how to turn those lemons into something useful. In this chapter, we're going to explore how to navigate setbacks, bounce back stronger, and even find a little humor in the chaos.

Step 1: Acknowledge the Suck

Let's start with the most important step: admitting that sometimes, life just sucks. There's no need to sugarcoat it or slap on a fake smile. You're allowed to feel frustrated, angry, or disappointed. In fact, you should. Suppressing those feelings doesn't make them go away, it just gives them a VIP pass to come back later when you least expect it.

Take a moment to acknowledge how you're feeling. Write it down, scream into a pillow, or have a good cry if you need to. (Pro tip: Ugly crying is more effective when paired with a dramatic playlist. Bonus points if it includes Adele.)

Acknowledging the suck isn't about wallowing, it's about giving yourself permission to feel human. And once you've done that, you can start figuring out your next move.

Step 2: Reframe the Situation

Now that you've let it all out, it's time to reframe those lemons. This doesn't mean pretending everything is fine or gaslighting yourself into thinking, *"This is actually a blessing in disguise!"* No. Reframing is about finding a perspective that empowers you instead of leaving you stuck in victim mode.

Ask yourself:

- *What can I learn from this?*
- *Is there an opportunity hidden in this mess?*
- *How can I use this experience to grow or pivot?*

For example, let's say you didn't get the promotion you were hoping for. It sucks. But maybe it's an opportunity to reevaluate your goals, develop new skills, or even consider a career change. Reframing doesn't erase the pain, but it gives you a sense of agency—and that's a powerful thing.

Step 3: Focus on What You Can Control

Here's a hard truth: Most of what happens in your life is out of your control. You can't control the weather, other people's actions, or the fact that your favorite show just got canceled (still not over it, by the way). You can only control what you have control over, and it ain't much when you look at things.

But you *can* control how you respond. You can choose to dwell on the things you can't change, or you can shift your energy toward the things you *can*.

Make a list of everything that's within your control—your habits, your mindset, your next steps. Then focus on taking action in those areas. It's a small but powerful way to reclaim your sense of agency, even when everything feels chaotic.

Step 4: Find the Humor

Yes, it's possible to laugh in the face of adversity—eventually. Humor has a way of lightening the load, even in the darkest of times. It doesn't mean you're ignoring the seriousness of the situation; it just means you're refusing to let it crush your spirit.

Think about a time when something went so spectacularly wrong that it was almost funny. Maybe you tripped in front of your entire office. Maybe your DIY project turned into a Pinterest fail. At the moment, it felt awful, but looking back, you can't help but laugh.

Finding humor in your struggles doesn't minimize them, it humanizes them. It reminds you that life is absurd, and sometimes the best way to deal with it is to laugh at the ridiculousness of it all.

Step 5: Create a "Lemonade Plan"

Once you've processed your feelings, reframed the situation, and found a shred of humor in the chaos, it's time to get practical. What's your next move? How are you going to turn this mess into something meaningful?

Here's how to create your Lemonade Plan:

1. **Define the Problem**: What's the issue you're dealing with? Be specific.

2. **Identify Your Resources**: What tools, skills, or support systems do you have to tackle this problem?
3. **Set Small Goals**: Break the problem into manageable steps. Remember, baby steps still count.
4. **Take Action**: Start with one small, actionable step—anything that moves you closer to a solution.

Your Lemonade Plan doesn't have to be perfect. It just has to be a starting point.

Momentum During Setbacks

Setbacks have a sneaky way of killing momentum, but they don't have to. In fact, a well-handled setback can actually fuel your momentum if you approach it the right way.

Here's how:

- **Treat Setbacks as Speed Bumps**: They might slow you down, but they don't have to stop you. Adjust your pace and keep moving forward.
- **Celebrate Resilience**: Every time you bounce back from a setback, you're proving to yourself how strong and capable you are. That's worth celebrating.
- **Keep the Big Picture in Mind**: Remember why you started. Your goals are still valid, even if the path to achieving them looks a little different now.

The Power of Perspective

Let's talk about perspective for a minute. Sometimes, the best way to deal with life's lemons is to zoom out and look at the bigger picture.

Ask yourself:

- *Will this matter a year from now?*

- *What's one thing I'm grateful for, even in this situation?*
- *How can this experience shape me for the better?*

Perspective doesn't solve your problems, but it does make them feel a little less overwhelming. And sometimes, that's all you need to keep going.

Homework Time

Let's turn all this lemon talk into action. Here's your homework for this chapter:

1. **Throw a Lemon (Metaphorically)**: Identify one frustration or setback you're dealing with right now. Allow yourself to vent, scream, or ugly cry—whatever helps you process it.

2. **Reframe the Lemon**: Write down one lesson or opportunity hidden in this situation. (Yes, it's there. Keep digging.)

3. **Create Your Lemonade Plan**: Outline one small, actionable step you can take to start addressing the problem.

4. **Laugh About It**: Find one humorous aspect of the situation and share it with a friend, family member, or your journal.

Extra Thoughts

Life is messy, unpredictable, and sometimes downright unfair. But you're stronger than you think, and every setback is an opportunity to grow, learn, and adapt.

So, the next time life hands you lemons, throw them at a wall. Scream, laugh, and then pick yourself up and start making lemonade. Because you've got this.

Pause for Reflection:

Sometimes, we hold on so tightly to things—beliefs, regrets, expectations—that we fail to see the weight they add to our lives. Life is a delicate balance between holding on and letting go. Think of the rakes in your life, those things you cling to, whether it's a toxic habit, a past mistake, or a future expectation. The more you hold on to them, the more you walk through life feeling burdened. But what if the true freedom lies not in grasping at control but in releasing what no longer serves you? Take a moment and reflect—what are you still holding on to that is holding you back? What could you let go of today to move forward with more peace and clarity?

Step 6: Recruit Your Lemonade Crew

Look, sometimes you can handle life's lemons on your own. Other times, you need a team of expert lemonade-makers to help you out. Enter: your Lemonade Crew.

These are the people who lift you up when you're down, remind you of your strengths when you've forgotten them, and occasionally drag you out of your pity party and back into the real world.

Here's how to identify your crew:

1. **Find Your Cheerleaders**: These are the people who believe in you, even when you don't believe in yourself. They're the ones who say, *"You've got this!"* and mean it.

2. **Recruit Your Fixers**: Sometimes you need practical help—a mentor, a problem-solver, or someone with skills you lack. Fixers are great for brainstorming solutions and offering guidance.

3. **Lean on Your Listeners**: When you just need to vent, your listeners are there. They don't try to fix things; they just let you feel your feelings without judgment.

Your Lemonade Crew doesn't have to be big. Even one or two trusted people can make a world of difference. And don't forget—you can be someone else's crew, too. Imagine the things you will learn from helping others by being part of their Lemon Crew. Helping others with their lemons can be a surprisingly effective way to deal with your own.

Step 7: Use Your Lemons to Help Others

Here's a little secret about setbacks: They have a way of making you more empathetic, compassionate, and relatable. When you've been through the wringer, you're uniquely equipped to help others navigate their own challenges.

Think about it:

- Your breakup advice hits differently when you've survived heartbreak yourself.
- Your career wisdom is richer when you've weathered a layoff or a bad boss.
- Your humor is sharper when you've learned to laugh at your own missteps.

Using your lemons to help others doesn't just make the world a better place—it also gives your struggles purpose. It reminds you that even the worst experiences can lead to something meaningful.

Step 8: Give Yourself Permission to Rest

Sometimes, the best way to deal with life's lemons is to take a step back and rest. And no, this isn't the same as giving up. Resting is a strategy—a chance to recharge, regroup, and come back stronger.

Think of yourself as a phone battery. When you're drained, you're not much use to anyone (especially yourself). But when you take the time to recharge, you're better equipped to handle whatever comes your way.

Rest can take many forms:

- Taking a nap.
- Spending time in nature.
- Watching your favorite guilty-pleasure show.
- Journaling or meditating.
- Saying *no* to obligations that drain you.

Rest isn't lazy. It's necessary. So, if you're feeling overwhelmed, give yourself permission to hit pause. Your lemons will still be there when you're ready to tackle them—but you'll be tackling them with a clearer head and a stronger spirit.

The Art of Turning Lemons into Lemonade

Let's get philosophical for a second: What does it really mean to "make lemonade"? It's not about pretending everything is fine or glossing over the tough stuff. It's about finding a way to create something positive—or at least manageable—out of a tough situation.

Here are a few examples of lemonade-making in action:

- You lose your job, but you use the downtime to explore a new career path.
- You face rejection, but it pushes you to refine your skills or pivot your approach.
- You go through a tough breakup, but it leads to a deeper understanding of what you want (and deserve) in a relationship.

Making lemonade doesn't mean the lemons don't suck. It just means you refuse to let them define you.

Momentum Through Chaos

Here's the kicker: Even when life is throwing lemons at you like it's training for a fruit-based Olympic sport, you can still build momentum. Take the effort to learn something new, either online or from someone else. Learning a new skill can be valuable. It might look different—it might be slower, messier, and more chaotic—but it's still possible for you to succeed.

Here's how:

1. **Celebrate Micro-Wins**: When the big picture feels overwhelming, focus on the smallest possible victories. Did you get out of bed today? Win. Did you make a to-do list? Double win.

2. **Lean on Rituals**: During chaotic times, rituals provide a sense of stability. Even something as simple as your morning coffee routine can anchor you.

3. **Focus on Progress, Not Perfection**: Remember, momentum isn't about moving fast—it's about moving forward, no matter how slowly.

Homework Time: Lemon Edition

Let's put this chapter into action with a little hands-on homework:

1. **Identify Your Lemon**: What's one challenge or setback you're currently facing? Write it down.

2. **Create Your Lemonade Plan**: Outline one small, actionable step you can take to address the challenge. Remember, baby steps count!

3. **Recruit Your Crew**: Reach out to one person who can support you, whether it's a cheerleader, fixer, or listener.

4. **Find the Humor**: Write down one funny or absurd thing about the situation. If you can't laugh about it yet, that's okay—but keep this step in your back pocket for later.

Optional Homework Time:

1. **Let Go of One Limiting Belief:** Identify one belief that has held you back for years. It could be something like "I'm not good enough" or "I'll never succeed." Write it down and reflect on it. Then, take the first step toward letting it go. This could mean replacing the belief with an empowering one or taking action that directly contradicts the belief. The goal is to see it for what it is—just a belief, not a fact.

2. **Release One Thing:** Is there something physical you're holding onto because you think you "should" or "might need" it in the future? Maybe an item from your past, a pile of clutter, or something that reminds you of an old version of yourself? Let it go. This could be a small item or a larger one, but the idea is to make space, both physically and mentally, for what's to come.

3. **Emotional Detox:** Take a moment to reflect on a past emotion or experience that you've been carrying around. This could be resentment, guilt, or fear. Write it down, acknowledge it, and then release it. Let it go through an act of compassion, acceptance, or forgiveness. The point is to lighten your emotional load and create space for the present moment.

End of Chapter Exercises:

1. **Gratitude Release Exercise:** Spend five minutes listing things you're grateful for. As you write, think about how each of these things has shaped you, and then take a moment to "release" the ones that you no longer need to cling to. This could include past experiences, old relationships, or self-limiting thoughts. Afterward, close your eyes and take a deep breath, feeling the relief that comes from letting go of unnecessary weight.

2. **The Letting Go Ritual:** Find a small, symbolic way to release something you're ready to let go of. This could be writing a letter to someone you need to forgive and then burning it, giving away an item that no longer serves you, or simply saying goodbye to a thought or habit that's been weighing you down. The act itself isn't as important as the intention behind it: to release and move forward.

3. **Meditative Release:** Sit quietly and visualize a version of yourself holding a heavy sack. This sack contains all the things you've been carrying—fear, doubt, regrets, or expectations. One by one, begin to unload the sack. Imagine letting go of each burden until it's empty. When you finish, take a deep breath, and feel the lightness of letting go.

Key Takeaways:

- **Holding On Causes Pain:** Clinging to old beliefs, expectations, or experiences weighs you down. The more tightly you hold on, the more energy you lose in the process.

- **Letting Go Creates Space:** Releasing what no longer serves you creates room for growth, new experiences, and peace. By letting go, you make space for what's truly important.

- **Release Brings Freedom:** The freedom to move forward, to grow, and to embrace what's next. Letting go isn't about forgetting; it's about choosing what to carry with you and what to leave behind.

- **Forgiveness Is Key:** Whether it's forgiveness of others or yourself, releasing old emotional wounds is a powerful way to step into the present, free from the weight of the past.

- **The Power of Acceptance:** Accepting that some things are beyond your control allows you to release unnecessary tension and move forward with more ease.

Cheat Sheets & Recaps:

- **The Power of Letting Go:** Life becomes lighter when you release the things that weigh you down—whether that's physical clutter, emotional baggage, or old beliefs.

- **Emotional Detox:** Cleanse yourself of emotional toxins by consciously letting go of negative thoughts, anger, or guilt. Every time you do, you create more space for joy and peace.

- **Releasing Limiting Beliefs:** Beliefs that no longer serve you can trap you in a cycle of self-doubt. Let go of limiting beliefs, and replace them with empowering thoughts.

- **Forgiveness:** Forgiveness is not about the other person—it's about freeing yourself from the burden of holding onto resentment or anger.

- **The Letting Go Process:** Letting go isn't a one-time event; it's a continuous practice. Regularly check in with yourself and see what you're holding on to, then consciously release what no longer serves you.

Kenism: *"Each small win may seem insignificant, but when you string them together, you create a path of progress. The rakes in your life are not failures; they are victories in disguise. They are the moments that remind you to keep moving, to keep stepping forward, and to trust that the sum of small victories will eventually lead to great transformation. So, when you find yourself stepping on that rake, remember—it's just another small win in your journey. Celebrate it, learn from it, and take the next step with greater clarity."*

Final Thoughts

Life's lemons aren't fun. They're messy, sour, and occasionally painful. But they're also opportunities—chances to grow, adapt, and prove to yourself just how resilient you are.

So, the next time life hands you lemons, don't let them weigh you down. Throw them, squeeze them, laugh at them—do whatever you need to do. Then take a deep breath, make a plan, and start turning those lemons into something you can be proud of.

Now, give yourself a pat on the back (or a slice of lemon cake, if you're feeling fancy) for making it through another chapter. And get ready for Chapter 7, where we'll dive into the art of staying on track, even when the road gets bumpy.

TL;DR: Letting go is the key to freedom. Whether it's emotional baggage, limiting beliefs, or past experiences, holding on only weighs you down. In this chapter, you've learned the power of release. It's time to lighten your load—physically, mentally, and emotionally—and make space for the growth, peace, and clarity you deserve. By letting go, you free yourself to move forward with a lighter heart and a clearer mind.

Notes:

Chapter 7: Staying on Track (Even When You Want to Burn It All Down)

Kenism: *"Setbacks are not the end; they are a necessary pause. Just as a tree does not grow straight without the wind, your growth will not be a straight path. The rakes are there to teach you resilience—to show you how to rise again after every fall. Life will push you, sometimes harder than you can handle. But how you respond to the setback defines you. Do you rise with grace, or do you remain down, defeated? Remember, every setback is a lesson, a sign that you are growing stronger."*

First off, congratulations on making it to Chapter 7! You've been through a lot of self-discovery, some solid laughs, and maybe a few eye rolls at my expense. But here we are, ready to tackle the biggest challenge of all: staying on track.

Because let's be honest—starting is the easy part. Keeping the momentum going when life gets busy, stressful, or just plain boring? That's the real struggle. Staying on track requires resilience, discipline, and a good sense of humor (because, let's face it, life is going to throw some curveballs your way).

But here's the thing: Staying on track isn't about being perfect. It's about finding ways to keep moving forward, even when you're tempted to give up and binge-watch your way through an entire season of *whatever Netflix just dropped*. So, let's dive in.

Step 1: Remember Your "Why"

We've touched on this before, but your "why" is the foundation of everything. It's the reason you started this journey, the fuel that keeps you going when the road gets tough, and the light at the end of the tunnel when everything feels dark.

When you're struggling to stay on track, revisit your "why." Write it down, say it out loud, tattoo it on your forehead (okay, maybe don't do that). The point is to keep it front and center, so you're always reminded of what you're working toward.

Pro Tip: If your "why" feels a little fuzzy, try digging deeper. Instead of just saying, *"I want to get healthier,"* ask yourself, *"Why do I want to get healthier? What will that allow me to do?"* The more specific and personal your "why," the more powerful it becomes.

Step 2: Embrace the "Reset Button"

Let's get one thing straight: Falling off track doesn't mean you've failed. It just means you're human. Everyone—*and I mean everyone*—has moments when they lose focus, make mistakes, or feel like giving up. The key is not to let one bad day turn into a bad week, month, or year.

Think of staying on track like driving a car. If you take a wrong turn, you don't just abandon the car and declare the trip a failure. You pull over, check the map, and get back on the road.

Your reset button works the same way. Missed a workout? Hit reset. Ate an entire pizza by yourself? Hit reset. Forgot to work on your goals for a week? You guessed it—hit reset. The sooner you hit that button, the easier it is to get back on track.

Step 3: Build Fail-Safe Habits

Staying on track isn't about willpower—it's about systems. The more automatic your habits, the less effort it takes to stick with them. Think of habits as the safety nets that catch you when motivation runs out.

Here's how to build fail-safe habits:

1. **Start Small**: Focus on one tiny habit at a time. (Remember Chapter 3? Baby steps!)

2. **Anchor Your Habits**: Tie your new habit to an existing routine. For example, if you want to start journaling, do it right after brushing your teeth.

3. **Set Triggers**: Create reminders or cues that prompt your habit. Sticky notes, alarms, and visual cues are your friends here.

4. **Reward Yourself**: Celebrate your wins, no matter how small. Positive reinforcement makes habits stick.

Step 4: Plan for Obstacles

Newsflash: Life isn't going to make this easy for you. There will be distractions, temptations, and unexpected challenges that try to derail your progress. The best way to stay on track is to plan for those obstacles in advance.

Here's how:

- **Identify Your Triggers**: What situations or emotions are most likely to knock you off track?

- **Create a Plan**: Decide in advance how you'll handle those triggers. For example, if stress makes you reach for junk food, stock up on healthier snacks or take a quick walk instead.

- **Practice Self-Compassion**: When obstacles inevitably show up, don't beat yourself up. Acknowledge the setback, adjust your plan, and keep moving forward.

Step 5: Track Your Progress

There's something magical about tracking your progress. It makes your efforts visible, tangible, and—dare I say it—fun.

Here are a few ways to track your progress:

- **Journaling**: Write down your wins, challenges, and insights each day.
- **Habit Trackers**: Use a calendar, app, or even a sticker chart to mark off each day you stick to your goals.
- **Photo Logs**: Take pictures of your progress, whether it's a fitness journey, a decluttering project, or a creative endeavor.
- **Progress Check-Ins**: Schedule regular check-ins with yourself (or a buddy) to review how far you've come and adjust your goals as needed.

Tracking isn't just about measuring success—it's about celebrating the effort you're putting in. And that deserves recognition.

Step 6: Make It Fun

Here's a revolutionary idea: What if staying on track didn't have to feel like a chore? What if it could actually be—wait for it—fun?

Think about ways to inject joy, creativity, and humor into your journey:

- Turn your workouts into a dance party.
- Gamify your goals with rewards and challenges.

- Share your progress with friends who can cheer you on (or join in).
- Celebrate milestones with something that makes you happy.

When you enjoy the process, staying on track becomes less of a grind and more of an adventure.

Step 7: Build a "Bounce-Back" Toolbox

Even with the best intentions, there will be times when you feel like giving up. That's why you need a bounce-back toolbox—your go-to resources for reigniting your spark and getting back on track.

Here's what to include:

- **A Motivational Playlist**: Music that gets you pumped and reminds you of your badassery.
- **Inspiring Quotes**: Keep a list of quotes that resonate with you and revisit them when you need a boost.
- **Your "Why"**: Write it down, make it visual, and keep it somewhere you'll see it often.
- **Self-Care Rituals**: Activities that help you recharge, refocus, and reset.

Your toolbox is your secret weapon for staying resilient, even when the road gets rough.

Homework Time

Let's turn all this theory into action. Here's your homework for this chapter:

1. **Revisit Your "Why"**: Write it down in bold, big letters and stick it somewhere visible.

2. **Hit the Reset Button**: Identify one area where you've fallen off track and take one small step to get back on course.
3. **Build a Bounce-Back Toolbox**: Start assembling your go-to resources for staying motivated and resilient.
4. **Make It Fun**: Find one way to inject joy, creativity, or humor into your journey this week.

Pause for Reflection:

In the journey of life, we all encounter setbacks—those moments when the rake catches us off guard, and we fall. It is in these moments that resilience is born. Resilience is not about avoiding the rakes; it's about how you rise after they strike. Take a moment now to think: What recent setback have you faced? How did you respond? Did you sit there, defeated, or did you rise, dust yourself off, and keep moving forward? The true test of resilience is not how many times you fall, but how many times you get back up. In this chapter, we explore the essence of resilience and how to cultivate it in your life, so that when the rakes strike, you don't just survive—you thrive.

Step 8: Lean Into Your Community

When it comes to staying on track, your environment matters. And no, I don't just mean having a clutter-free desk or a well-stocked pantry (although those help). I mean the people around you—the ones who cheer you on, hold you accountable, and occasionally remind you to stop doomscrolling and get back to work.

Your community is your secret weapon. Whether it's a friend, a partner, a mentor, or a random person you met on the internet who shares your goals, having someone in your corner can make all the difference.

Here's how to lean into your community:

1. **Share Your Goals**: Tell someone about what you're working on. Saying it out loud makes it real and gives you an accountability buddy.
2. **Celebrate Together**: Share your wins—big or small—and let others cheer you on. (Yes, you deserve that applause for drinking water today!)
3. **Ask for Help**: Struggling to stay on track? Reach out. People love helping, and you'll be surprised at the support you get when you're honest about your needs.

Pro Tip: If you don't have a built-in support system, find one. Join a group, a class, or an online community that aligns with your goals. There's strength in numbers, and you don't have to do this alone.

Step 9: The Magic of "Non-Negotiables"

Let's talk about non-negotiables—the things you commit to doing no matter what. Non-negotiables are the backbone of staying on track. They're the small but mighty actions that keep you grounded, even when everything else feels chaotic.

Here's how to create your non-negotiables:

1. **Keep It Simple**: Choose 1–3 actions that are easy to maintain, even on your busiest days.
2. **Make Them Meaningful**: Your non-negotiables should align with your goals and values. For example, if health is a priority, drinking water might be a non-negotiable.
3. **Be Flexible**: Non-negotiables aren't about perfection. If you can't hit your usual target, aim for a scaled-down version.

Examples of non-negotiables might include:

- Drinking one glass of water every morning.
- Moving your body for five minutes a day.

- Writing down one gratitude before bed.

The key is to make these habits so ingrained that they become second nature to you. Something that you learn to do daily, on the regular. Something that become automagic for you to just do, not to think, but just do. Yes, I said automagic, that so you can see the magic of consistency.

Step 10: Master the Art of Recalibration

Even with the best intentions, life happens. Plans change, routines get disrupted, and some days you feel like you're spinning plates while riding a unicycle on a tightrope. This is where recalibration comes in.

Recalibration is about adjusting your approach without abandoning your goals. Think of it like steering a ship—sometimes you need to correct your course to stay on track.

Here's how to recalibrate:

1. **Evaluate What's Working**: Take a moment to reflect on what's going well and what isn't.
2. **Adjust Your Goals**: If a goal feels overwhelming or unrealistic, scale it back. Progress is still progress, no matter how small.
3. **Set a New Plan**: Map out your next steps, focusing on small, actionable changes.
4. **Start Fresh**: Treat each day as a new opportunity to get back on track.

Recalibration isn't about starting over—it's about staying flexible and adapting to life's inevitable curveballs.

Step 11: Reward Yourself Along the Way

Let's be real: Staying on track can feel like a grind sometimes. That's why rewards are so important. They give you something to look forward to, celebrate your hard work, and make the journey a little more fun.

But here's the catch: Your rewards should enhance your progress, not sabotage it. For example, if your goal is to eat healthier, your reward shouldn't be an all-you-can-eat junk food buffet. Instead, treat yourself to a new cookbook, a fancy kitchen gadget, or a meal at your favorite healthy restaurant.

Here are some reward ideas to get you started:

- A guilt-free movie night.
- A new book, journal, or planner.
- A relaxing bubble bath with candles and music.
- A small splurge on something you've been eyeing (but within reason).

Remember, rewards aren't just for big milestones. Celebrate the small wins, too. You're building momentum, and that deserves recognition.

Step 12: Cultivate Patience

This one's a doozy, so buckle up: Progress takes time.

We live in a world of instant gratification, where everything from Amazon Prime deliveries to viral TikToks promises quick results. But real, meaningful change? That's a slow burn. It's the result of consistent effort, day in and day out.

When you're tempted to throw in the towel because you're not seeing results fast enough, remember this: The tortoise always beats the hare. Your progress might be slow, but it's steady—and that's what matters.

Cultivate patience by focusing on the process instead of the outcome. Trust that every small step you take is moving you closer to your goal, even if you can't see the results yet.

Homework Time

Let's turn all this staying-on-track wisdom into action. Here's your homework for this chapter:

1. **Set Your Non-Negotiables**: Choose 1–3 simple habits that you'll commit to every day, no matter what.

2. **Recruit a Buddy**: Reach out to someone who can cheer you on, hold you accountable, or just remind you why you started.

3. **Recalibrate Your Goals**: Take a moment to evaluate your progress and adjust your approach as needed.

4. **Plan a Reward**: Choose a small reward for sticking to your goals this week. (Hint: Make it something that genuinely makes you happy.)

Optional Homework Time:

1. **Reframe Your Setback:** Think of a recent setback that left you feeling defeated or frustrated. Write it down, then reframe it. How can you see this setback as an opportunity for growth? Perhaps it taught you patience, resilience, or the importance of persistence. Write down three lessons that this setback taught you, and reflect on how you can apply them moving forward.

2. **Resilience Action Plan:** Identify an area in your life where you need more resilience. It could be a difficult project at work, a personal challenge, or a recurring habit you want to break. Break down your plan into small, manageable steps, and focus on one at a time. For each step, write down a potential obstacle and how you will overcome it. This will help

you build the mental and emotional muscles needed to handle challenges with grace.

3. **Strengthen Your Mind:** Resilience isn't just about physical endurance; it's about mental toughness. Spend 10 minutes a day in meditation, visualization, or affirmations that reinforce your belief in your ability to persevere. Visualize yourself overcoming obstacles with ease and confidence, strengthening your internal resilience.

End of Chapter Exercises:

1. **Resilience Journal:** Each day for the next week, write about one instance where you showed resilience, no matter how small. This could be bouncing back from a tough conversation, sticking with a task even when it was difficult, or choosing to stay calm in a stressful situation. After writing, reflect on how this builds your resilience.

2. **Set a Resilience Goal:** Identify a goal that requires you to push through discomfort or adversity. It could be anything from starting a fitness routine to confronting a fear. Write down your goal and the specific challenges you expect to encounter. Create an action plan for handling those challenges with resilience.

3. **Resilience Meditation:** Find a quiet place and close your eyes. Visualize yourself as an oak tree, rooted deeply in the earth, standing tall through a storm. As you breathe, imagine each gust of wind (representing a challenge) bending you, but never breaking you. Feel the strength and resilience building within you as you connect to the core of your being.

Key Takeaways:

- **Resilience Is Built Through Adversity:** It's easy to be resilient when things are going well, but true resilience is forged in the fire of adversity. It is the ability to bounce back stronger every time life knocks you down.

- **Setbacks Are Not Failures:** Every setback is simply a setup for a comeback. You don't lose when you fall; you learn how to rise.

- **Resilience Is a Skill, Not a Trait:** Anyone can develop resilience. It's a skill that you build by confronting difficulties, learning from them, and choosing to continue despite them.

- **Rise Stronger:** It's not about how many times you fall, but how many times you rise. Resilience is about the mental and emotional muscle you build each time you face a challenge.

- **Your Response Is Your Power:** Your resilience lies not in what happens to you, but in how you respond to what happens. Choose to rise, choose to move forward, and choose to thrive.

Cheat Sheets & Recaps:

- **Resilience Is the Key to Growth:** Every obstacle is an opportunity to become stronger. When life throws a rake in your path, use it to learn and build resilience.

- **Setbacks Are Stepping Stones:** See every failure or setback as a chance to grow. The more you encounter, the more you learn how to deal with them gracefully.

- **Resilience Can Be Developed:** It's not about how tough you are naturally, but about how you respond and grow from difficult experiences. Practice resilience daily.

- **Embrace Discomfort:** True resilience is developed when you step into discomfort and adversity. It's about staying committed to your growth, no matter the obstacles.

- **Self-Belief Fuels Resilience:** The stronger your belief in your ability to bounce back, the more resilient you will be. Reinforce that belief with every challenge you overcome.

Kenism: "When you embrace setbacks, you see them not as failures but as moments of growth. The rake that strikes you isn't punishment; it is an invitation to develop resilience, patience, and awareness. As you encounter obstacles in your path, ask yourself, 'What is this moment teaching me?' The answer will shape your journey forward. So, do not avoid the setbacks, but embrace them with an open heart, knowing that each one is simply a step in your evolution."

Final Thoughts

Staying on track isn't about being perfect. It's about learning to get back up, dusting yourself off, and to keep moving forward. It's about finding the balance between discipline and compassion, effort and rest, structure and spontaneity. Showing up, adapting, and celebrating small wins are what it's all about. It's about trusting the process, even when it feels slow, and remembering that consistency beats intensity every time.

You've got this, my friend. You've got everything you need to keep going. The tools, the mindset, and—most importantly—the resilience to handle whatever comes your way. So, take a deep breath, give yourself a high five, and get ready for the next chapter.-You're building a life that aligns with your goals, your values, and your unique version of success. And if you ever feel like you're losing your way, just revisit this chapter, hit the reset button, and keep moving forward.

Now, take a deep breath, give yourself a well-deserved high five (or a snack—always a good choice), and get ready for Chapter 8. The journey continues, and you're already doing better than you think.

The journey continues, and you're crushing it.

TL;DR: Resilience is your superpower. It's not about avoiding challenges; it's about how you respond to them. Every setback is a chance to grow stronger. With resilience, you'll bounce back from anything life throws at you, learning valuable lessons along the way. Practice resilience by embracing discomfort, learning from setbacks, and keeping your focus on growth.

Notes:

Chapter 8: The Setback Symphony—Embracing the Chaos

Kenism: *"We hold onto many things in life—ideas, beliefs, expectations. But holding on too tightly is like walking down the path while stepping on every rake in sight. We cling to things that cause us pain, not realizing that letting go is the key to freedom. When you let go, you stop resisting life, and you begin to move with it. The rakes will still be there, but you will walk around them, with more ease and less tension. Let go of what weighs you down, and you will find that the path ahead is clearer than you ever imagined."*

Congratulations, my resilient friend. You've tackled motivation, momentum, failure, and staying on track like a total pro. Now it's time for the ultimate challenge: setbacks.

Setbacks are the unwelcome guests at the party of life. They show up uninvited, knock over the punch bowl, and linger just long enough to ruin the vibe. But here's the thing about setbacks: they're inevitable. No matter how carefully you plan or how hard you work, life is going to throw you a curveball—or twelve.

The good news? Setbacks don't have to derail your progress. In fact, they can be some of the most valuable, transformative moments of your journey—if you know how to handle them. In this chapter, we're going to dive into the art of embracing chaos, pivoting with grace, and turning setbacks into stepping stones.

Step 1: Redefine What Setbacks Mean

Let's start with a reframe. Most people see setbacks as failures—proof that they're not cut out for success. But that's not what setbacks are. Setbacks are *data points.* They're feedback from the universe, telling you that something needs to change, pivot, or adjust.

Think of it this way: If you're driving to a new destination and miss a turn, you don't give up and go home. You reroute. Setbacks work the same way. They're not the end of the road; they're just a detour.

Pro Tip: The next time you hit a setback, try asking yourself, *"What is this trying to teach me?"* The answer might surprise you.

Step 2: Allow Yourself to Feel the Feels

Let's get one thing straight: It's okay to feel frustrated, disappointed, or even downright angry when a setback happens. You're not a robot (and if you are, I've got questions). Ignoring your emotions doesn't make them go away, it just buries them until they resurface at the worst possible time.

So, give yourself permission to feel the feels. Cry, vent, punch a pillow, or scream into the void if you need to. Just make sure you don't unpack and live there. Feel it, process it, and then start moving forward.

Step 3: Identify the Root Cause

Not all setbacks are created equal. Some are external—things beyond your control, like a global pandemic or your favorite coffee shop running out of oat milk. Others are internal—habits, beliefs, or patterns that keep tripping you up.

When you hit a setback, take a moment to dig deeper. What caused it? Was it something outside your control, or is there something within your power to change? Identifying the root cause helps you figure out your next steps and prevents the same setback from happening again.

Step 4: Pivot Like a Pro

Here's the thing about setbacks: They often require you to change course. And while change can be scary, it's also an opportunity to get creative, try new approaches, and discover solutions you might not have considered before.

Think of setbacks as plot twists in the story of your life. Sure, they weren't part of the original script, but they make things a whole lot more interesting. Plus, some of the best moments in life come from unexpected detours.

When you're faced with a setback, ask yourself:

- *What's the next best step I can take?*
- *Is there another way to approach this goal?*
- *What resources, tools, or support can I use to pivot?*

Step 5: Keep the Big Picture in Mind

Setbacks have a way of making you lose sight of the big picture. Suddenly, all you can see is the problem in front of you, and it feels like the end of the world. But here's the truth: It's not.

Zoom out and remind yourself why you started this journey in the first place. Your goals, your values, and your "why" are still valid, even if the path to achieving them looks a little different now.

Pro Tip: When you're feeling stuck, take a moment to visualize your end goal. Close your eyes, imagine what success looks like, and let that vision reignite your motivation.

Step 6: Build Your Resilience Muscle

Resilience isn't something you're born with—it's a skill you build over time. And setbacks are the perfect training ground.

Every time you bounce back from a setback, you're strengthening your resilience muscle. You're proving to yourself that you can handle whatever life throws your way, and that's a powerful thing.

Here are a few ways to build resilience:

1. **Practice Self-Compassion**: Be kind to yourself, especially when things don't go as planned.
2. **Focus on Gratitude**: Even in the midst of a setback, there's always something to be grateful for.
3. **Reframe the Narrative**: Instead of seeing setbacks as failures, view them as opportunities to learn and grow.

Step 7: Find the Silver Lining

Okay, I know this one sounds a little *too* optimistic, but hear me out. Every setback has a silver lining—it just might take a little digging to find it.

Maybe a missed opportunity pushes you to pursue something even better. Maybe a tough lesson makes you stronger, wiser, or more empathetic. Or maybe the silver lining is simply that you survived the setback and lived to tell the tale.

The point isn't to sugarcoat your struggles—it's to remind yourself that even the worst situations can lead to growth, insight, and unexpected blessings.

Step 8: Stay Consistent (Even When It's Hard)

Setbacks have a sneaky way of making you want to throw in the towel. But consistency is the antidote. Even when progress feels slow, even when motivation is nowhere to be found, showing up—no matter how imperfectly—is what keeps you moving forward.

Here's a secret: Consistency doesn't mean doing everything perfectly. It means doing *something,* no matter how small. A five-minute workout, a single journal entry, or one healthy meal still counts.

Consistency is what turns setbacks into comebacks.

Homework Time: Turning Setbacks Into Stepping Stones

Let's turn this chapter into action. Here's your homework:

1. **Reframe a Recent Setback**: Think of a setback you've faced recently. Write down what happened, what you learned, and how you can pivot.

2. **Identify the Silver Lining**: Find one positive takeaway from the setback—no matter how small—and write it down.

3. **Plan Your Next Step**: Choose one small, actionable step to move forward.

4. **Practice Resilience**: Reflect on a time when you bounced back from a tough situation. Use that memory as proof of your strength.

Pause for Reflection:

Patience. It's often seen as a passive virtue—waiting, holding back, doing nothing while life passes by. But patience is not about idly waiting for things to happen. It's about trust. It's about accepting the natural rhythm of life and understanding that things unfold in their own time. When we rush, we often miss the lessons that come with the waiting. Think about the times when you've felt impatient—what was it that made you feel that way? Were you rushing to reach a destination, or were you trying to avoid discomfort? Take a moment to reflect: What would happen if you practiced patience in your life, especially in the moments when you're most tempted to rush? Would the rakes still get in your way, or would you learn to see them from a distance and avoid them?

Step 9: Make Peace with Imperfection

Let's have a moment of honesty: You're not perfect. And guess what? That's okay. Perfection is overrated, unattainable, and honestly, a little boring. The good stuff in life—the growth, the learning, the moments that make you laugh until you cry—comes from imperfection.

When setbacks happen, it's easy to fall into the trap of perfectionism. You think, *"If I can't do this perfectly, why bother?"* But here's the truth: Progress isn't about perfection. It's about showing up, doing your best, and embracing the messy, glorious process of being human.

Here's how to embrace imperfection:

1. **Focus on the Effort, Not the Outcome**: Celebrate the fact that you tried, regardless of the result.
2. **Find the Beauty in the Mess**: Imperfection is what makes life interesting. Lean into it.
3. **Give Yourself Grace**: Treat yourself with the same kindness and understanding you'd offer a friend.

Pro Tip: The next time you catch yourself spiraling into perfectionism, remind yourself: *Done is better than perfect.*

Step 10: Turn Setbacks Into Stories

Every setback is a story waiting to be told. And let's be real, some of the best stories come from the worst disasters. How many times have you been glued to the edge of your seat as someone tells a genuinely good story about a setback they had. You're like, "Oh no, tell me more… then what?"

Think about it. What's more interesting:

- A tale of smooth sailing, where everything goes according to plan?
- Or a dramatic saga of struggles, mishaps, and eventual triumph?

Exactly.

When you're in the middle of a setback, it might feel like the end of the world. But one day, you'll look back and laugh. You'll tell the story of how you accidentally emailed your boss instead of your best friend, or how your first attempt at baking a cake ended with a fire alarm.

Stories are how we make sense of setbacks. They remind us that life is absurd, unpredictable, and—most importantly—temporary. So, start collecting your stories. They're the breadcrumbs that lead you through the forest of chaos.

Step 11: Build a Setback Survival Kit

If setbacks are inevitable, why not prepare for them in advance? Think of it like packing an emergency kit for life's curveballs.

Here's what to include in your Setback Survival Kit:

1. **Your "Why"**: A written reminder of why you started and what you're working toward.
2. **Encouraging Notes**: Write yourself a pep talk or collect messages from friends who believe in you.
3. **Quick Wins**: A list of small, manageable actions that help you rebuild momentum.
4. **Comfort Items**: A favorite book, playlist, or snack that brings you comfort and joy.

5. **A Reminder of Past Resilience**: A journal entry, photo, or memento from a time when you overcame a challenge.

Keep your survival kit somewhere accessible, so it's ready to go when you need absolutely it.

Step 12: Laugh in the Face of Chaos

When setbacks hit, humor can be your secret weapon. It's hard to feel defeated when you're busy laughing at the absurdity of it all.

Did you miss a deadline because you got distracted by a YouTube rabbit hole? Classic. Did your DIY project turn into a Pinterest fail of epic proportions? Iconic.

Laughter doesn't solve problems, but it makes them a whole lot easier to handle. It shifts your perspective, lightens the load, and reminds you that life doesn't have to be so serious.

Pro Tip: Keep a "Setback Hall of Fame" where you document your funniest, most ridiculous failures. Over time, it becomes a reminder of how far you've come—and a source of endless entertainment.

Step 13: Celebrate Your Comebacks

Here's the thing about setbacks: They make comebacks possible. Every time you bounce back from a challenge, you're proving to yourself that you're stronger, wiser, and more capable than you thought.

So, don't just focus on the setback—celebrate the comeback. Take time to acknowledge your resilience, your effort, and your growth. You've earned it.

Celebration ideas:

- Treat yourself to something you love—a fancy coffee, a new book, a movie or dinner out, or even just a guilt-free nap.
- Share your win with a friend who'll cheer you on.

- Write about your comeback in your journal, so you can revisit it when you need a confidence boost.

Celebrating your comebacks isn't just about feeling good, it's about reinforcing the belief that you can handle whatever life throws your way.

Step 14: Keep Moving Forward

At the end of the day, the most important thing you can do after a setback is to keep moving forward. Even if it's slow, even if it's messy, even if you're not entirely sure where you're going, just keep going.

Progress isn't about speed or perfection. It's about resilience, persistence, and the courage to take one more step, no matter how small.

So, take a deep breath, dust yourself off, and get back in the game. Because you're not just surviving setbacks, you're turning them into stepping stones for something greater.

Homework Time: Embrace the Chaos

Ready to turn setbacks into stepping stones? Here's your homework:

1. **Create Your Setback Survival Kit**: Gather the tools, reminders, and comfort items that will help you navigate tough times.

2. **Reframe a Recent Setback**: Write down what happened, what you learned, and how you're bouncing back.

3. **Celebrate a Comeback**: Reflect on a time when you overcame a challenge and do something to celebrate your resilience.

4. **Start Your Setback Hall of Fame**: Document your funniest or most ridiculous setbacks as a reminder of your ability to laugh and move forward.

Optional Homework Time:

1. **Embrace Waiting:** Think of something in your life that you've been impatient about—whether it's a goal, a project, or even something as simple as waiting in line. For the next week, whenever impatience arises, instead of trying to rush through it, try sitting with the discomfort. Embrace the waiting. Write down your feelings and how your perspective shifts when you allow yourself to simply wait, without anxiety.

2. **Patience Challenge:** Pick a task this week that you usually rush through, whether it's a simple chore or a long-term project. This time, do it with full attention, taking it slow and savoring the process. No multitasking. Be present in the moment, and practice patience as you complete the task. Reflect afterward on the difference it made.

3. **Mindful Breathing:** When you feel your impatience rising, stop and take five deep breaths. Inhale slowly through your nose, hold, and exhale through your mouth. With each breath, remind yourself that there's no need to rush. This exercise will help you regain control over your impatience and center yourself in the present moment.

End of Chapter Exercises:

1. **Patience Reflection Journal:** Write about a time when patience served you well. Maybe it was waiting for a project to come to fruition or letting a relationship evolve at its own pace. Reflect on how you felt during that time and what you learned about the power of waiting. The goal here is to find your patience in action and understand how it benefits you.

2. **Create a Patience Plan:** Identify an area of your life where you're struggling with impatience. Is it with work, relationships, or personal growth? Create a step-by-step plan for practicing patience in that area. Be specific: What are some moments where you need to stop, breathe, and let things unfold at their own pace? Write down your plan, and commit to it for the next week.

3. **The Waiting Game:** Choose something you normally rush through (e.g., eating, doing the dishes, etc.). This week, practice slowing down and savoring the experience. How does it feel to give each task your full attention, rather than rushing through it just to get it done?

Key Takeaways:

- **Patience Is Active, Not Passive:** Patience isn't about doing nothing—it's about choosing to trust the process and allow things to unfold naturally. It's an active decision to stay calm and focused while waiting.

- **Impatience Creates Stress:** Rushing through life's tasks can create unnecessary stress and lead to mistakes. Practicing patience allows you to make better decisions and enjoy the process, not just the outcome.

- **Timing Is Everything:** Life has its own rhythm. When you try to rush things, you often miss the subtle moments that matter most. When have you forced things and it's gone well? Not ever or at least not many times. Sometimes the timing isn't right. Trust that everything will happen in its time.

- **Patience Leads to Greater Wisdom:** The more you practice patience, the more you realize that things usually turn out better when you let them unfold naturally. You gain insight and understanding by resisting the urge to push things too quickly.

- **Patience Is a Skill to Be Developed:** Like any other skill, patience requires practice. It's not about waiting passively but about becoming more mindful and conscious of your thoughts, actions, and reactions in the face of discomfort.

Cheat Sheets & Recaps:

- **Patience Is Power:** The art of waiting with awareness is a skill that will help you navigate life's challenges with ease. Stop rushing and start savoring the journey.

- **Impatience Is a Barrier to Clarity:** When you're impatient, you make decisions based on anxiety, not clarity. Patience allows you to see the bigger picture.

- **Time and Timing:** Understand that not everything happens on your timeline. Allow space for things to unfold and trust in the natural process of life.

- **The Practice of Presence:** In every moment of impatience, there is an opportunity to practice presence. Instead of rushing to the next thing, focus on where you are right now.

- **Slow Down to Speed Up:** The more patient you are, the more efficient you will become. Slowing down allows for more mindful action, fewer mistakes, and better outcomes.

Kenism: "The more you hold on, the more you step on the rakes. Letting go is not about abandoning responsibility; it is about releasing unnecessary weight. You cannot move forward with clenched fists, for there is no space to receive what life has to offer. So, release your grip on old habits, limiting beliefs, and outdated stories. Allow yourself to walk lightly, without fear of the rakes, knowing that when you let go, the world opens up in ways you cannot yet imagine."

Final Thoughts

Setbacks aren't the end of the road—they're part of the journey. They're the plot twists that make life interesting, the detours that lead to unexpected destinations, and the challenges that shape you into the resilient, unstoppable badass you're meant to be.

So, the next time life hands you a setback, remember this: You've got the tools, the mindset, and the humor to handle it. Feel the feels, embrace the chaos, and keep moving forward. Because every step you take is a step toward the life you're building—and it's going to be amazing.

Now, take a moment to celebrate the fact that you just conquered another chapter. High five, fist bump, or victory snack—your choice. And get ready for Chapter 9, where we dive into the art of making this momentum last for the long haul.

TL;DR: Patience is not about waiting idly; it's about trusting the process and allowing things to unfold naturally. When you practice patience, you reduce stress, improve decision-making, and find more joy in the journey. The key to overcoming impatience is learning to be present and embrace the moment—trust that everything will happen in its own time.

Notes:

Chapter 9: How to Make the Momentum Last

Kenism: *"Patience is not the ability to wait; it is the ability to stay calm while waiting. Just as the tree waits for the seasons to change, you too must learn to wait for your time. The rakes will be there, no matter how much you rush. But when you step too quickly, without awareness, you are bound to fall. Patience teaches us to trust the timing of life, to understand that everything unfolds when it is meant to. When you stop rushing, you stop stepping on the rake."*

Momentum is a lot like a spark. It's exhilarating when it first ignites, lighting up your path and making you feel unstoppable. But if you don't nurture it, that spark can fade into a flicker—and eventually, a frustrating pile of ash.

So, how do you keep the momentum alive? How do you turn that initial burst of energy into a steady, sustainable fire that keeps you moving forward, even when life gets messy, boring, or downright hard?

That's what this chapter is all about. Together, we're going to build a momentum maintenance plan that works for *you*. Think of it as a long-term strategy for being your best, most productive, least-binge-watching-TikTok-until-3-a.m. self.

Step 1: The Secret Sauce of Consistency

Here's the deal: Momentum thrives on consistency. It doesn't need flashy grand gestures or dramatic leaps forward. What it needs is your commitment to showing up, day after day, even when you don't feel like it.

Imagine momentum as a plant. You don't have to drench it with water or give it a pep talk every day (though, honestly, it wouldn't hurt). You just need to water it consistently, a little at a time, and trust that it'll grow.

How to Build Consistency:

1. **Start Tiny**: Go back to those baby steps from earlier chapters. Consistency is born from actions so small they feel almost effortless.

2. **Create Routines**: Tie your habits to existing routines so they become automatic.

3. **Track Your Progress**: Use a journal, app, or calendar to visually mark your wins.

Pro Tip: If you miss a day, don't sweat it. Missing one day won't derail your momentum, but letting guilt or perfectionism keep you from restarting will.

Step 2: Stay Curious, Not Complacent

Momentum dies when you get complacent. If you're always doing the same things, the spark that got you excited in the first place can start to dim. That's why it's crucial to stay curious, keep experimenting, and challenge yourself to grow. When you experiment, try new things, explore your options, you have a tendency to stay on task and to keep on building your momentum.

Ways to Keep Things Fresh:

- Try a new approach to an old goal.
- Learn a skill that complements what you're already working on.
- Set micro-challenges for yourself (like "no phone for the first hour of the day" or "try one new recipe this week").

Curiosity isn't just about avoiding boredom—it's about discovering new layers of motivation and momentum you didn't know you had.

Step 3: Make Rest Part of the Plan

Momentum doesn't mean running at full speed 24/7. In fact, the fastest way to kill your momentum is to burn yourself out. That's why rest isn't just important, it's essential.

Think of rest as the fuel that keeps your engine running. Without it, you're just going to sputter, stall, and curse at life in general.

How to Rest Without Guilt:

1. **Schedule It**: Plan regular breaks, downtime, or "nothing" days where you can recharge guilt-free.
2. **Redefine Productivity**: Remember that rest *is* productive. It's what allows you to show up fully when it matters most.
3. **Listen to Your Body**: Pay attention to signs of burnout—like irritability, exhaustion, or wanting to chuck your laptop across the room—and take action before you hit a wall.

Step 4: Build a Momentum Maintenance Team

We talked about building your Lemonade Crew back in Chapter 6, but now it's time to upgrade them into your Momentum Maintenance Team. These are the people who keep you accountable, inspired, and on track for the long haul.

Who's On Your Team?

1. **The Cheerleader**: The friend who hypes you up no matter what.
2. **The Challenger**: The person who pushes you to aim higher and avoid coasting.
3. **The Mentor**: Someone who's walked this path before and can offer guidance.
4. **The Accountability Buddy**: The person who calls you out (lovingly) when you start slipping.

Pro Tip: Be intentional about communicating your goals to your team. Let them know how they can support you and what you need to stay motivated.

Step 5: Celebrate the Journey

Momentum thrives on positivity. When you take time to celebrate your progress, you reinforce the belief that your efforts matter—and that's a powerful motivator to keep going.

How to Celebrate Without Sabotaging:

1. **Acknowledge Small Wins**: Don't wait for big milestones to celebrate. Every step forward deserves recognition.
2. **Choose Rewards That Align**: Pick rewards that enhance your progress, like new workout gear for hitting a fitness goal or a day trip to recharge your creativity.
3. **Reflect on Growth**: Take time to look back on where you started and how far you've come.

Celebrating isn't just about feeling good, it's about fueling your momentum with gratitude and pride. And you don't need a major party for every accomplishment. But you can celebrate in small ways that make you acknowledge your success and learnings.

Step 6: Be Your Own Coach

Here's a wild thought: What if you started treating yourself like someone you care about?

Too often, we're our own worst critics. We nitpick, berate, and hold ourselves to impossible standards. But when you're building momentum, that inner critic can be your biggest saboteur.

How to Be a Better Coach to Yourself:

1. **Use Positive Self-Talk**: Replace harsh criticism with encouragement. Instead of saying, *"I'm so lazy,"* try, *"I'm doing the best I can, and I'm proud of that."*
2. **Focus on Solutions**: When setbacks happen, shift your energy from blame to problem-solving.
3. **Practice Self-Compassion**: Remember, progress isn't linear, and you're allowed to have bad days.

Pro Tip: Write a letter to yourself as if you were your own coach. What advice, encouragement, or tough love would you offer?

Step 7: Stay Flexible, Stay Focused

Life is unpredictable, and even the best momentum maintenance plans will need to be adjusted. The key is to stay focused on your goals while remaining flexible in your approach.

How to Balance Flexibility and Focus:

1. **Revisit Your Goals Regularly**: Are they still aligned with your values? Do they still excite you?
2. **Adapt to Challenges**: When obstacles arise, don't abandon your goals—find new ways to approach them.

3. **Keep Your Eyes on the Prize**: No matter how many detours you take, remember why you started this journey in the first place.

Homework Time

Let's make sure your momentum stays unstoppable. Here's your homework:

1. **Schedule Rest**: Block out time in your calendar for guilt-free rest and recovery.

2. **Build Your Team**: Identify the people who can support your momentum and let them know how they can help.

3. **Celebrate Progress**: Pick one recent win—big or small—and find a meaningful way to celebrate it.

4. **Write a Self-Coaching Letter**: Offer yourself advice, encouragement, and motivation to keep going.

Pause for Reflection:

Life is full of moments where we feel tethered—by expectations, fears, or even the past. We often carry around these emotional weights, believing they are necessary for survival. But what if, in reality, they are the very things holding us back? Think of the rakes in your life—not just the physical ones, but those emotional or mental rakes that keep getting in your way. These are the grudges, the regrets, the "what-ifs" that we cling to. Take a moment now to reflect: What are you holding onto? What could you release to create more space for freedom? Letting go isn't about forgetting or abandoning; it's about making room for something new to enter your life. The first step toward that freedom is recognizing what no longer serves you and making the choice to release it.

Step 8: Reinvent Yourself When Necessary

Momentum doesn't mean clinging to the same path forever. Sometimes, staying on track requires you to pivot, adapt, and even reinvent yourself. All of us have had to reinvent ourselves after failure or even success. This isn't failure, it's evolution, it's welcomed change.

Think about it: You're not the same person you were five years ago. Your priorities, goals, and values have shifted, and that's a good thing. Embracing change allows you to stay aligned with what truly matters to you.

Signs It's Time to Reinvent:

- You're no longer excited about your goals.
- Your progress has stalled, and you feel stuck.
- Life circumstances have changed, and your old plan no longer fits.

How to Reinvent Without Losing Momentum:

1. **Reevaluate Your Goals**: Ask yourself if they still align with your current values and aspirations.
2. **Set Fresh Intentions**: Create new goals or adjust existing ones to reflect who you are now.
3. **Keep the Essentials**: Hold onto the habits, routines, and lessons that still serve you, and let go of the rest.

Reinvention isn't about starting over; it's about leveling up.

Step 9: Remember the Power of Gratitude

Gratitude is one of the simplest, most effective ways to keep momentum alive. Why? Because it shifts your focus from what's missing to what's working. It reminds you of how far you've come, the resources you have, and the people who've supported you along the way.

How to Cultivate Gratitude:

1. **Start a Gratitude Journal**: Write down three things you're grateful for each day. They don't have to be big—sometimes, "I didn't spill coffee on myself today" is enough. Sometimes, "I remembered to take out the recycling this morning" works.

2. **Express Appreciation**: Tell the people in your life how much they mean to you. Gratitude is contagious.

3. **Celebrate the Present**: Instead of constantly chasing the next goal, take time to appreciate where you are right now.

Gratitude doesn't just make you feel good, it reinforces the belief that you're capable of achieving even more.

Step 10: Stay Inspired

Momentum thrives on inspiration. When you're feeling stuck or unmotivated, reconnect with the things that inspire you.

Where to Find Inspiration:

- **Books and Podcasts**: Find resources that challenge your thinking and expand your perspective.
- **Role Models**: Learn from people who've achieved what you're working toward.
- **Nature**: Take a walk, hike, or just sit outside and let the natural world reset your mindset.
- **Creative Outlets**: Sometimes the best way to reignite your spark is to do something creative—write, paint, dance, or try something completely new.

Inspiration is like fuel for your fire. Keep adding it, and your momentum will keep growing.

Step 11: Know When to Rest, Reset, and Recharge

Let's talk about the holy trinity of sustainable momentum: rest, reset, and recharge. These aren't signs of weakness, they're essential tools for staying in the game.

Rest: This is your time to recharge your physical and mental energy. Rest days aren't optional, they're a requirement for long-term success.
Reset: When things feel off, take a step back and reevaluate. Resetting isn't about starting over; it's about recalibrating.
Recharge: Find activities that refill your cup, whether it's spending time with loved ones, exploring a hobby, or indulging in some much-needed alone time.

Momentum doesn't mean pushing yourself to the brink. It means knowing when to pause so you can come back stronger.

Step 12: Keep the Fire Burning

Here's the truth about momentum: It's not about never losing the spark—it's about knowing how to reignite it.

When the excitement fades or the road gets tough, remember why you started. Revisit your goals, lean on your support system, and take one small step forward. Progress is built in the moments when it feels hardest to keep going.

And when you stumble (because you will), remind yourself that momentum isn't about perfection. It's about persistence. The simple act of showing up, again and again, is what keeps the fire burning.

Homework Time:

1. **Release a Grudge:** Think of a person or situation you're holding a grudge against. Write down how this grudge makes you feel and what it has cost you emotionally. Then, make a conscious decision to let it go. You don't have to forgive them right away, but commit to releasing the weight of this grudge

from your life. Write a letter to that person, not to send, but to express your feelings and finally let them go.

2. **Clear the Clutter:** Look around you—physically and mentally—and identify things you're holding onto that no longer serve you. It could be an old possession, a bad habit, or an outdated belief. Take action today by letting go of at least one thing. Physically clean out a drawer, delete old emails, or remove an item from your life that's no longer aligned with who you want to become.

3. **Forgiveness Exercise:** Consider a past situation that you have not fully forgiven. Whether it's forgiving someone else or yourself, write down your thoughts and feelings about this situation. Then, write down what forgiveness looks like for you in this situation. It may not be instantaneous, but the act of reflecting and acknowledging your power to forgive is the first step in letting go.

End of Chapter Exercises:

1. **Mindful Release:** Set aside 10 minutes each day for the next week to practice mindful release. This could be through meditation, deep breathing, or journaling. Focus on letting go of a different thought, memory, or item each day. With each release, imagine yourself becoming lighter, more focused, and more open to new opportunities. After you've done it for a week, continue this practice weekly. Do this so you reset your mindset and have learned to release the negative.

2. **Letting Go of Negative Thought Patterns:** Identify one negative thought pattern you have (e.g., "I'm not good enough" or "I'll never be successful"). Write it down and counter it with a positive affirmation. For example, replace "I'm not good enough" with "I am worthy of success." Practice

this affirmation daily for the next week, allowing it to slowly replace the old thought pattern.

3. **Symbolic Letting Go Ritual:** Create a ritual that symbolizes letting go. This could involve writing down things you need to release, burning the paper, and watching the smoke dissipate. Or, perhaps burying something (a symbol, a note, etc.) as a representation of releasing the past and stepping forward into freedom.

Key Takeaways:

- **Letting Go Is Liberating:** Holding on to things, whether they're material possessions or emotional baggage, weighs you down. Letting go frees up energy and makes room for new possibilities.

- **Forgiveness Is for You, Not Them:** Forgiveness doesn't mean condoning harmful behavior; it means releasing the hold that past hurts have on your life. Forgiveness is a gift you give yourself.

- **Clutter Blocks Clarity:** Physical clutter often mirrors emotional or mental clutter. When you let go of things that no longer serve you, you create space for what truly matters.

- **Release Creates Space for Growth:** Just as a tree drops its leaves to make way for new growth, releasing old, unhelpful patterns and possessions opens up space for your next chapter.

- **Embrace the Flow of Life:** When you stop clinging to the past, you allow life to flow through you. You move with more ease and grace, unaffected by old patterns or memories.

Cheat Sheets & Recaps:

- **Letting Go Is an Active Choice:** To release something, you must consciously decide to let it go. It's not a passive act—it requires effort, intention, and the willingness to move forward.

- **Forgiveness Heals:** You don't need to forget to forgive. Forgiveness is about releasing the burden of negative emotions and freeing yourself from the past.

- **Space Equals Freedom:** Whether it's emotional, mental, or physical, creating space is key to moving forward. The more you let go, the more freedom you gain and the more you will move forward successfully.

- **Clutter Is a Sign of Resistance:** Holding on to things (physical, emotional, or mental) is often a sign that we are resisting change. Let go, and you create the space for transformation.

- **Small Acts of Release:** Releasing doesn't have to be dramatic. Small acts of letting go, like clearing clutter or shifting thought patterns, accumulate over time to create big changes.

Kenism: *"Patience is not about passivity—it is about active waiting. When you are patient, you are aligned with the natural flow of life. You understand that each step forward, no matter how small, is important. The rakes in your life are not obstacles to rush past, but opportunities to practice patience, to stay calm and centered in the face of challenges. So, the next time you step forward, do so with patience and presence. Trust that the path will unfold exactly as it is meant to."*

Closing Thoughts

You've made it to the end of Chapter 9, which means you're officially a momentum master. You've learned how to build it, sustain it, and adapt when life throws you curveballs. Most importantly, you've proven to yourself that you're capable of more than you ever thought possible.

Remember: Momentum isn't a onetime thing. It's lifelong practice, a commitment to showing up for yourself and your goals, no matter what. And the best part? You're not doing this alone. You've got the tools, the mindset, and the resilience to keep moving forward—and I'll be right here, cheering you on every step of the way.

Momentum isn't something you achieve once and then forget about. It's a living, breathing thing that requires care, attention, and a willingness to adapt. But the good news? You've got everything you need to make it last.

So, keep showing up. Keep experimenting, celebrating, and resting when you need to. And most importantly, keep believing in yourself. Because the life you're building is worth it—and so are you.

Now, take a deep breath, pat yourself on the back, and get ready for Chapter 10. We're about to bring everything together and finish this journey with a bang. Give yourself a well-deserved round of applause (or a cupcake, because you've earned it), and get ready for the grand finale, the best is yet to come, my friend.

TL;DR: Letting go is the key to freedom. Whether it's emotional baggage, negative thought patterns, or physical possessions, holding on only weighs you down. In this chapter, you learned that forgiveness, decluttering, and making space for growth are essential to moving forward. Let go of what no longer serves you, and you'll free yourself to embrace new opportunities and a clearer path ahead.

Notes:

Chapter 10: The Big Picture—Crafting a Life That Feels Like Your Own

Kenism: *"Resilience is not simply the ability to bounce back—it is the ability to grow from the struggle. Each time you step on a rake, you are faced with a choice: to fall or to rise. Resilience is the quality that enables you to rise, no matter how many rakes lie in your path. It is the inner strength to bend without breaking, to learn from each setback, and to keep going when the way is unclear. Like the bamboo that bends in the wind but does not break, resilience allows you to flow with life's challenges and emerge stronger."*

Welcome to Chapter 10, my friend. This is the grand finale, the victory lap, the place where everything comes together. You've battled through motivation slumps, setbacks, and the chaos of life with grit, humor, and maybe a few snacks along the way. Now it's time to zoom out and look at the big picture: *your life.*

This isn't about creating a Pinterest-perfect version of success or living up to anyone else's expectations. It's about crafting a life that feels like your own—a life that aligns with your values, celebrates your quirks, and makes you excited to wake up in the morning (most mornings, anyway; let's not set unrealistic expectations here).

So, let's roll up our sleeves and get to work. We're going to design a life that doesn't just survive the ups and downs but thrives in them.

Step 1: Define Success on Your Terms

Here's the thing about success: It's a shape-shifter. Society, social media, and your nosy aunt at Thanksgiving all have their own ideas about what it should look like. But the only definition that matters is yours.

Take a moment to ask yourself:

- *What does success mean to me?*
- *How do I want to feel in my life, not just look on the outside?*
- *What are the things I value most—things I wouldn't trade for anything?*

For some, success is climbing the corporate ladder. For others, it's having time to travel, paint, or binge-watch *The Great British Bake Off* guilt-free. Whatever it is, own it. There's no wrong answer here, as long as it's true to you.

Step 2: Map Out Your Priorities

Once you've defined success, it's time to figure out how to get there without losing your mind—or your soul. Take out a piece of paper and map out your priorities. Look up ways you can mind-map, many of us learned mind mapping in junior high school and learned them again while take a note taking class in college or other higher education. This starts with identifying your top priorities.

Think of your life as a jar. Your priorities are the big rocks, the things that matter most. The smaller, less important stuff—like emails, errands, or whether or not your neighbor mows their lawn on time—

are the pebbles and sand. If you fill your jar with sand first, there's no room for the rocks. But if you prioritize the rocks, the smaller stuff will find its place.

How to Find Your Big Rocks:

1. **List Your Values**: What do you care about most? Family? Creativity? Health? Adventure?

2. **Evaluate Your Time**: Are you spending your energy on what matters, or is it getting sucked into distractions?

3. **Set Boundaries**: Say no to the things that don't align with your priorities, even if it feels uncomfortable at first.

Pro Tip: Check in with yourself regularly. Your priorities may shift over time, and that's okay.

Step 3: Embrace Imperfect Balance

Let's bust a myth right here: Perfect balance doesn't exist. Life isn't a scale where everything stays perfectly aligned; it's more like a seesaw, constantly shifting as you juggle work, relationships, hobbies, and the occasional existential crisis.

The goal isn't to achieve balance, it's to embrace it. Some weeks, work will take center stage. Other weeks, you'll need to focus on rest or personal growth. The key is to stay flexible and keep the big picture in mind.

How to Embrace Balance:

- **Plan Your Weeks with Intention**: Decide where your energy is needed most and adjust accordingly. And that energy need could change daily. It may not change for a month or a week, you get to decide.

- **Forgive Yourself for Dropping the Ball**: It happens to everyone. The trick is to pick it back up.

- **Celebrate the Small Wins**: Even tiny moments of balance (like squeezing in a 10-minute walk) count. Oh, you paid off a credit card, time to congratulate yourself.

Step 4: Build Joy into Your Routine

Life isn't just about grinding toward goals—it's about enjoying the journey. That's why building joy into your daily routine is non-negotiable. Joy isn't frivolous; it's fuel.

How to Add More Joy:

1. **Identify Your Joy Triggers**: What makes you smile, laugh, or feel at peace? (Hint: If it involves puppies, you're not alone.)

2. **Schedule Time for Fun**: Put it on your calendar like you would a work meeting.

3. **Celebrate Playfulness**: Try something silly or new, like karaoke, a painting class, or a spontaneous road trip.

Pro Tip: Joy isn't just about big moments. It's also about savoring the little things—like a perfectly brewed cup of coffee or a great song on the radio.

Step 5: Find Meaning in the Mess

Life is messy. Even with the best-laid plans, there will be curveballs, detours, and days when you feel like you're walking through molasses. The trick is to find meaning in the mess.

Ask yourself:

- *What am I learning from this?*
- *How can this experience shape me into the person I want to become?*
- *What story will I tell about this someday?*

Finding meaning doesn't mean ignoring the hard stuff. When you attack the messiness of life, those difficult things we all hate to do like taxes, seeding the lawn, building a fence, etc. It means choosing to believe that even the messiest moments have something to teach you.

Step 6: Leave Space for the Unknown

Here's a plot twist for you: You don't have to have it all figured out. In fact, some of the best things in life come from the unexpected—the opportunities you didn't plan for, the people you didn't expect to meet, the passions you didn't know you had.

Leave space in your life for the unknown. Be open to new experiences, say yes to things that scare you, and trust that not knowing the whole plan is part of the adventure.

Pro Tip: When in doubt, remind yourself that every great story starts with uncertainty. Embrace it—it's where the magic happens.

Homework Time: Designing Your Life

Let's put this all into action. Here's your homework for this chapter:

1. **Define Your Success**: Write down what success looks and feels like for you. Be specific.

2. **Identify Your Big Rocks**: List your top priorities and evaluate whether your time reflects them.

3. **Plan a Joy Boost**: Schedule one activity this week that brings you pure, unfiltered joy.

4. **Embrace the Unknown**: Write down one thing you're curious about exploring, even if it feels scary or uncertain.

Pause for Reflection:

Resilience isn't a skill you're born with; it's a muscle you build over time. Life will never be smooth, and the rakes will always be there, just waiting to spring up and catch you. But it's not the rakes that determine your journey—it's how you respond to them. Think about the toughest challenge you've faced in recent months. What did it teach you about yourself? Did you give up, or did you dig deeper and rise stronger? Resilience is about getting knocked down and choosing to rise again, no matter how many times it takes. Pause for a moment to reflect on how far you've come in your life. Every obstacle you've overcome has shaped the resilient person you are today. Now ask yourself—what could you become if you embraced every challenge as an opportunity to grow?

Step 7: Surround Yourself with Good Energy

You've heard it before, but it bears repeating: You are the average of the five people you spend the most time with. If your circle is filled with naysayers, energy vampires, and people who still think it's okay to double dip at parties, you're going to struggle to thrive.

The people you surround yourself with matter. They shape your mindset, influence your decisions, and either lift you up or drag you down. So, it's time to do an audit of your inner circle.

How to Build a High-Vibe Circle:

1. **Find the Builders**: These are the people who support your dreams and help you brainstorm solutions when things get tough.

2. **Seek Out Joy Spreaders**: You know those people who radiate positivity and make you laugh until your stomach hurts? Keep them close.

3. **Look for Mentors**: Surround yourself with people who inspire you, challenge you, and make you want to be better.

4. **Set Boundaries with Energy Drainers**: It's okay to limit time with people who bring negativity into your life.

Pro Tip: If you don't have the support system you need right now, start building it. Join groups, attend events, or even connect online. Your people are out there—they're just waiting for you to find them.

Step 8: Create Your Legacy in Real Time

Let's get deep for a second: What do you want your legacy to be?

I'm not talking about how the world remembers you when you're gone—I'm talking about the impact you're making right now, in this moment. Every action you take, every relationship you nurture, and every decision you make contributes to your legacy.

Ask yourself:

- *How do I want the people around me to feel after spending time with me?*
- *What kind of example do I want to set for others?*
- *What am I doing today that aligns with the mark I want to leave on the world?*

Your legacy isn't a someday thing. It's happening now, with every choice you make. So, make them count.

Step 9: Practice Gratitude for the Journey

By now, you've probably noticed a recurring theme in this book: gratitude. That's because it's one of the most powerful tools for creating a life that feels fulfilling, grounded, and joyful.

Gratitude isn't just about saying "thank you" or jotting down a few things in a journal (though those are great starts). It's about training your brain to focus on abundance instead of scarcity, growth instead of setbacks, and the beauty of the present moment instead of the what-ifs of the future.

How to Make Gratitude a Daily Habit:

1. **Start Your Day with Gratitude**: Before you even get out of bed, think of one thing you're grateful for.
2. **End Your Day with Gratitude**: Reflect on the day and identify three moments that made you smile, laugh, or feel appreciated.
3. **Express It**: Tell someone you're grateful for them. It'll make their day—and yours, too.

Gratitude doesn't just make you happier; it also keeps your momentum alive by reminding you of all the reasons to keep moving forward.

Step 10: Trust Yourself

If there's one takeaway I want you to carry from this book, it's this: *You can trust yourself.*

You've proven, chapter after chapter, that you're capable of overcoming challenges, embracing growth, and building a life you're proud of. You don't need anyone's permission to chase your dreams, pivot your plans, or live authentically. You've got this.

When self-doubt creeps in (and it will), remind yourself of all the times you've succeeded, grown, and learned from your mistakes. Trust that you have the tools, the resilience, and the creativity to handle whatever comes next.

The Journey Continues

As you turn the final pages of this book, I want you to take a moment to reflect on how far you've come. You've built momentum, navigated setbacks, and learned to embrace the messiness of life with humor, heart, and a healthy dose of sarcasm. That's no small feat.

But here's the thing: This isn't the end of your journey. It's just the beginning. The road ahead is yours to design, and it's filled with endless possibilities, surprises, and opportunities to grow.

You've got the blueprint, the mindset, and the determination to create a life that feels like your own. And I, for one, can't wait to see where it takes you.

Homework Time: Wrapping It All Up

To close this chapter (and this book!) on a high note, here's your final homework:

1. **Write Your Success Story**: Take a moment to reflect on what you've accomplished so far and what you're most proud of. Write it down—it's worth celebrating.

2. **Set One Big, Bold Goal**: Dream big. What's one goal that scares you a little but excites you a lot? Write it down and commit to taking one small step toward it today.

3. **Pay It Forward**: Share what you've learned with someone else. Whether it's a friend, a family member, or a stranger on the internet, your story has the power to inspire.

4. **Celebrate Yourself**: Seriously. You've earned it. Treat yourself to something that makes you happy, whether it's a fancy dinner, a new book, or a guilt-free Netflix binge.

Homework Time:

1. **Resilience Reframing:** Think of a recent setback or challenge that felt like a failure. Write it down, and then reframe it. Instead of viewing it as a loss, focus on what you learned from it. How did it make you stronger, wiser, or more determined? This exercise helps you shift from victimhood to empowerment.

2. **Build Your Resilience Plan:** Identify an area in your life where you need to build more resilience. It could be related to work, a personal goal, or overcoming fear. Write down the steps you'll take to build that resilience—whether it's through

small, consistent actions or developing a new mindset toward challenges.

3. **Resilience Affirmations:** Write down three affirmations that reinforce your resilience. For example, "I am capable of overcoming any challenge," or "I bounce back stronger from adversity." Repeat these affirmations every morning for the next week. This practice will train your mind to focus on strength, rather than weakness.

End of Chapter Exercises:

1. **Resilience Reflection Journal:** Spend 10 minutes each day reflecting on a time when you faced a challenge and overcame it. It doesn't have to be a huge victory; it could be something small, like pushing through a difficult workday or standing firm in a conversation. Reflect on how you showed resilience in that moment and how you can apply that same strength in future challenges.

2. **Resilience Visualization:** Take 5-10 minutes each day to visualize yourself handling challenges with grace and strength. Imagine a future obstacle, and see yourself rising to meet it with confidence and calmness. Visualizing your resilience will prime your mind to approach challenges with a sense of power rather than fear.

3. **Resilience Action Steps:** Identify one challenge you're currently facing—big or small. Break it down into actionable steps, and create a plan to tackle it. Think of this as your personal resilience boot camp. Each small step is a victory in itself, and the more steps you take, the more resilient you become.

Key Takeaways:

- **Resilience Is a Skill, Not an Inherited Trait:** Resilience isn't something you're born with; it's a muscle that grows with practice. The more you face adversity, the stronger you become.

- **Failure Is Not the End:** Every failure is an opportunity to learn, grow, and build resilience. The key is not to stay down but to rise each time you're knocked down.

- **Resilience Builds Strength Over Time:** It's the accumulation of small, everyday acts of perseverance that create a resilient mindset. Every challenge you face strengthens your emotional, mental, and physical resilience.

- **Mindset Matters:** Your ability to be resilient is deeply tied to your mindset. Embrace challenges as opportunities for growth, and your resilience will flourish.

- **Take Action, Even in Fear:** Resilience is built through action. Even when you're scared or unsure, take that first step forward. The act of moving through fear is what strengthens your resilience.

Cheat Sheets & Recaps:

- **Resilience Comes from Action:** You build resilience by moving through challenges, not by avoiding them. Every small act of courage contributes to your overall strength.

- **Perseverance is Key:** When faced with difficulties, remember that perseverance is your greatest asset. Push through the discomfort, and you'll come out stronger on the other side.

- **Failure Is Just Feedback:** View every setback as feedback. It's not an end, but a new beginning. Each failure offers valuable lessons that make you more resilient.

- **Growth Happens Outside Your Comfort Zone:** Resilience is developed when you step outside your comfort zone and face challenges head-on. This is where true growth happens.

- **Actionable Resilience:** Build resilience by taking small, consistent actions. The more action you take, the stronger your resilience muscle becomes.

Kenism: *"Resilience is not something you are born with, but something you cultivate through experience. With every rake that strikes you, you become more adaptable, more capable of handling whatever life brings. Remember, it is not the number of rakes on the path that determines your journey, but your ability to keep walking, to keep learning, and to keep rising. Life's challenges are not there to defeat you, but to make you stronger. Embrace the rakes, for they are the very things that will help you build the resilience you need to thrive."*

Final Thoughts

You've done it. You've made it through the twists, turns, and snarky commentary of this book, and you're standing at the edge of something incredible: a life that feels like your own. This book might be coming to an end, but your journey is just getting started. You have everything you need to create a life that feels fulfilling, joyful, and uniquely yours.

So, go out there and make it happen. Take the lessons, the laughter, and the occasional snark from these pages and use them to build momentum, navigate challenges, and keep moving forward. And when you stumble (because you will), remember: You're resilient, resourceful, and capable of so much more than you realize.

This isn't the end of your journey—it's the beginning. You have the tools, the mindset, and the resilience to keep growing, learning, and thriving. So, take a deep breath, trust yourself, and start crafting the life you've always wanted.

Close this book, take a deep breath, and get ready to create something amazing. You've got this—and I'll be cheering you on every step of the way. Now, go out there and make it happen. And remember: I'm rooting for you, every step of the way.

TL;DR: Resilience is your ability to rise from every challenge stronger than before. It's not about avoiding failure, but about learning from it and persevering. In this chapter, we explored how resilience is built over time, through consistent actions and a growth mindset. The more you practice resilience, the more you will thrive in the face of adversity. Every setback is a chance to grow—embrace it, learn from it, and keep moving forward with strength.

Notes:

Conclusion: The Last Chapter, but Just the Beginning

Kenism: *"The path to growth is not a smooth one. It is littered with rakes, obstacles, and moments of uncertainty. But what if I told you that these very challenges are the ones that shape you into who you are meant to become? The rakes are not your enemy. They are your teachers, guiding you toward deeper awareness and understanding. The only way to truly walk freely is to stop fearing the rakes and start learning from them."*

Well, here we are. The final chapter. If this were a Netflix series, the dramatic music would be kicking in right about now. But since this is your life, let's skip the melodrama and get straight to the heart of it: You've done something remarkable.

You've spent the past 10 chapters digging deep, challenging yourself, and (hopefully) laughing a little along the way. You've explored what it means to create momentum, navigate setbacks, and build a life that feels authentic, joyful, and meaningful. That's not just progress, it's transformation.

But here's the kicker: This isn't the end. This book might be wrapping up, but your journey is just getting started. You've laid the foundation, gathered the tools, and lit the spark. Now it's time to take everything you've learned and apply it to the rest of your life.

What You've Learned (and Why It Matters)

Before we officially close the book (pun intended), let's take a moment to reflect on what you've accomplished:

1. **You've Learned to Start**: You've discovered the power of tiny, imperfect steps and the magic of simply showing up.
2. **You've Faced Failure Head-On**: You've redefined failure as feedback and used setbacks as steppingstones.
3. **You've Built Momentum**: You've learned how to keep moving forward, even when motivation takes a vacation.
4. **You've Embraced Resilience**: You've proven that you can handle life's curveballs with grit, grace, and a sense of humor.
5. **You've Designed a Life That Feels Like Your Own**: You've mapped out your priorities, embraced joy, and crafted a vision of success that's true to you.

These lessons aren't just words on a page, they're tools you carry with you, no matter what challenges or opportunities come your way.

The Power of Small Wins

If there's one thing I hope you take away from this book, it's the importance of small wins. The little moments, the tiny victories, the everyday acts of showing up—they're the building blocks of a life well-lived.

Think about it:

- Every time you took a baby step, you proved to yourself that progress is possible.

- Every time you celebrated a win, you reinforced the belief that your efforts matter.
- Every time you bounced back from a setback, you built the resilience to keep going.

Small wins might not feel flashy or groundbreaking, but they add up. They're the breadcrumbs that lead you to bigger goals, deeper growth, and a life that feels meaningful.

So, keep celebrating those small wins. They're your secret weapon for creating lasting change.

Momentum Is a Lifelong Practice

Momentum isn't something you achieve once and then forget about—it's a lifelong practice. It's about showing up, day after day, even when the road gets bumpy or the spark starts to fade.

Here's the good news: You've already built the foundation. You know how to start, pivot, and keep going, no matter what life throws your way.

How to Keep the Momentum Alive:

1. **Stay Curious**: Keep learning, experimenting, and challenging yourself to grow.
2. **Stay Flexible**: Embrace change as an opportunity, not a setback.
3. **Stay Kind**: Treat yourself with compassion and celebrate every step forward, no matter how small.

Momentum isn't about perfection—it's about persistence. And you've got that in spades.

What Happens Next?

So, what's next for you? That's entirely up to you.

Maybe you're ready to tackle a big, bold goal that scares you a little. Maybe you're focused on finding joy in the everyday moments. Or maybe you're just taking it one step at a time, trusting that each action will lead you closer to the life you want.

Whatever path you choose, know this: You're capable of more than you realize. You've proven it to yourself chapter after chapter, step after step. And the best part? You're just getting started.

Pause for Reflection:

As we come to the end of this journey together, let's take a moment to pause and reflect. You've learned a lot about rakes—those inevitable moments of failure, setbacks, and challenges. But more importantly, you've learned that the rakes are not here to defeat you; they are here to teach you. The real question is not whether you will face rakes in your future, but how you will handle them. Will you let them stop you in your tracks, or will you rise each time, stronger and wiser? Take a breath, and ask yourself: How will you approach life's rakes moving forward? What lessons will you carry with you, and how will you use them to walk a path of resilience, patience, and awareness? The journey doesn't end here, it's only just beginning.

The Legacy of Your Efforts

As you step into the next chapter of your life (the real one, not this book), it's worth reflecting on something important: The effort you've put in doesn't just impact you. It ripples out into the world in ways you might not even realize.

Every time you take a step forward—no matter how small—you're setting an example. You're showing the people around you what's possible. You're proving that growth, resilience, and momentum are not just buzzwords; they're the building blocks of something extraordinary.

Think about it:

- When you work on yourself, you bring more patience, compassion, and joy to your relationships.
- When you chase your dreams, you inspire others to chase theirs.
- When you bounce back from a setback, you remind everyone watching that failure isn't the end—it's a new beginning.

Your efforts matter, not just to you but to everyone who crosses your path. That's the legacy you're building right now, in real time.

You Are Not Alone

Let's take a moment to acknowledge something important: This journey isn't one you've taken alone. You've leaned on friends, mentors, and maybe even complete strangers who've offered a kind word, a piece of advice, or a much-needed laugh along the way.

And that's exactly how it should be.

Life isn't meant to be a solo expedition. It's a team sport, a collaboration, a beautifully messy web of connections that make the hard stuff a little easier and the good stuff a lot sweeter.

So, as you move forward, remember to lean on your people. Ask for help when you need it, celebrate your wins with those who cheer you on, and pay it forward by being that source of support for someone else.

Because while this book might be about you and your journey, the truth is, we're all in this together.

The Gift of Progress

Here's the thing about progress: It's not just about getting closer to your goals. It's about who you become along the way.

Every step you've taken, every challenge you've faced, every time you've chosen to keep going instead of giving up—you've been shaping yourself into a stronger, wiser, more resilient version of you. And that's the real gift of progress.

So, the next time you're tempted to focus solely on the finish line, take a moment to appreciate the journey. Celebrate the fact that you're growing, learning, and evolving every single day.

Because the truth is, the journey *is* the destination.

A Few Final Words of Wisdom

Before we part ways, I want to leave you with a few final reminders, little nuggets of wisdom to carry with you as you write the next chapter of your story:

1. **You Are Capable**: There's no limit to what you can achieve when you commit to showing up for yourself.

2. **Progress Isn't Linear**: There will be twists, turns, and detours, but every step forward—no matter how small—matters.

3. **Joy Is Non-Negotiable**: Make time for the things that make your heart sing. Life is too short not to.

4. **You Are Enough**: Just as you are, right now. You don't need to prove your worth to anyone, including yourself.

The Beginning of Something Beautiful

As you close this book, I want you to remember one thing: This isn't the end. It's the beginning of something beautiful—a life that feels like your own.

You now have the tools, the mindset, and the momentum to create something extraordinary out of what you've learned here. So, take a deep breath, trust yourself, and step boldly into the future you're building.

The road ahead will not always be smooth, but it will be yours. Own it, learn from it and build on your mistakes while learning to laugh from them. And that, my friend, is what makes it worth traveling.

Homework Time:

1. **Revisit Your Rakes:** Think back to some of the biggest rakes you've stepped on in your life. What did you learn from each one? Now, look at your current path—what rakes are in front of you? How can you approach them with more awareness, humor, and resilience? Write down your reflections and action steps for dealing with any potential rakes on the horizon.

2. **Build Your Resilience Toolbox:** You've learned the importance of resilience in this book, so now it's time to actively build your resilience toolkit. Write down at least five strategies or practices that you can use to stay strong when challenges arise. These might include mindfulness, positive affirmations, seeking support from others, or simply taking a moment to pause and breathe before reacting.

3. **Create a "Rake-Free" Action Plan:** In the spirit of being proactive, think of one area in your life where you can become more aware and prevent future rakes. Whether it's a habit you want to change or a challenge you want to approach differently, create a plan to avoid stepping on that particular rake again. Set specific goals and actions that will help you navigate that area with greater clarity and presence.

One Last Optional Homework Assignment

Don't worry, this one's easy. As you finish this book, take a moment to do the following:

1. **Write Yourself a Love Letter**: Yes, really. Remind yourself of everything you've accomplished and why you're proud of the person you're becoming.

2. **Make a Promise**: Commit to continuing this journey, even when it gets tough. Write down one promise you're making to yourself and keep it somewhere visible.

3. **Celebrate**: Seriously. You've come so far. Treat yourself to something that brings you joy, whether it's a fancy dinner, a long nap, or a solo dance party in your living room.

End of Chapter Exercises:

1. **Resilience Review:** Look back over the exercises and lessons you've completed in this book. Write down the ones that have had the most impact on you and why. Which practices have already started to shift your mindset, and where do you still need more growth? Use this review as a reminder of how far you've come and where you still want to go.

2. **The Rake-Free Day:** Choose one day this week to approach life with complete awareness. Pay attention to your thoughts, actions, and reactions. The goal is to live without stepping on any rakes—be mindful of your choices and observe how it feels to avoid the things that have previously tripped you up. At the end of the day, journal about your experience and how awareness has changed your approach.

3. **Mindful Gratitude:** Create a daily practice of mindfulness and gratitude. Take a moment each day to reflect on the positive things in your life, especially the lessons you've learned from your rakes. This exercise will help you cultivate a mindset of appreciation and resilience, making you more prepared for whatever comes next.

Key Takeaways:

- **Rakes Are Part of Life's Journey:** Life will always present challenges, but those challenges aren't meant to break you.

They're meant to help you grow. The rakes in life are part of the process, shaping you into a stronger, wiser version of yourself.

- **Resilience Is the Key to Moving Forward:** The real power lies not in avoiding rakes, but in how you rise when they strike. Every setback is a lesson, and each lesson makes you more resilient.

- **Patience and Awareness Help You Navigate Life:** Patience isn't about waiting idly—it's about trusting the process and being present in the moment. When you combine patience with awareness, you can spot the rakes ahead and avoid unnecessary pain.

- **Letting Go Frees You to Move Forward:** Letting go of past mistakes, limiting beliefs, and old baggage is essential to moving forward. The more you release, the lighter and freer you become, ready to face whatever comes next.

- **You Are the Author of Your Journey:** The rakes you encounter are not what define you. It's your response to them, your ability to rise, learn, and grow, that shapes your journey. You have the power to move forward with clarity, resilience, and a sense of humor.

Cheat Sheets & Recaps:

- **The Rake is a Teacher:** Every challenge is an opportunity to learn and grow. Instead of avoiding the rakes, embrace them as teachers that guide you to greater understanding.

- **Resilience Is a Practice:** Build your resilience by facing challenges head-on. It's not about how many times you fall—it's about how many times you rise, stronger and more determined.

- **Patience and Awareness Are Essential:** Practice patience in the face of uncertainty. When you are present and aware, you can navigate life's challenges with ease.

- **Let Go to Move Forward:** Release what no longer serves you. Whether it's past regrets, limiting beliefs, or emotional baggage, letting go creates space for new opportunities.

- **You Control the Narrative:** Life may throw rakes in your path, but you control how you respond. Choose to learn, choose to rise, and choose to move forward with clarity and resilience.

A Final Word

Writing this book has been an absolute joy—not because of the words on the page, but because of what they represent: the courage, determination, and resilience it takes to build a life that feels like your own.

If there's one thing I want you to remember as you close this book, it's this: You're enough, just as you are. You don't need to be perfect, have all the answers, or achieve every goal overnight. You just need to keep showing up, keep trying, and keep believing in yourself.

Because the life you're building is worth it. And so are you.

Now, go out there and create something amazing. The world is waiting, and I, for one, can't wait to see what you do next.

My Final Wish for You

As you move forward, my wish for you is this:

- That you continue to show up for yourself, day after day.
- That you find joy in the journey, even when it's messy.
- That you trust in your ability to navigate whatever life throws your way.

- And that you never stop believing in the incredible, unstoppable, beautifully imperfect person you are.

Now, go out there and create something amazing. The world is waiting—and it's lucky to have you in it.

Kenism: *"As you move forward in life, remember that the rakes will always be there. They are not signs of failure, but moments of growth. Each strike is an opportunity to reflect, to learn, and to choose a different path. Life will always throw challenges your way, but how you respond is what defines your journey. So, the next time you step on a rake, don't fear the pain—embrace the lesson. With each step forward, you will find more clarity, more peace, and more strength. And in the end, you will walk through this world with a calm, steady mind, knowing that the rakes of life are not here to harm you, but to teach you the art of resilience."*

TL;DR:

Life is full of rakes, but they aren't here to stop you—they're here to teach you. Each challenge you face is an opportunity for growth. In this book, you've learned how to embrace failure, practice patience, let go of the past, and build resilience. The real key to moving forward is in how you respond to life's rakes—take them as lessons, laugh at the absurdity, and rise stronger each time. Your journey is yours to create, and with the tools you've learned here, you can navigate life with clarity, humor, and strength.

Notes:

FAQs/FAFs: Frequently Asked Questions/Fails

Welcome to the FAQ/FAF section, where I answer all the burning questions you probably didn't ask, but I know you're thinking anyway. The negative thoughts rolling around in your brain, the self-doubt, the imaginary concerns that hold you back more than you realize. This is the part of the book where I lovingly (and sarcastically) address your doubts, excuses, and what-ifs.

So, buckle up buttercup and let's tackle these one by one in an entertainingly fun and educational manner.

Kenism: *"In life, we all ask questions—some are simple, some are profound, but they all arise from our curiosities, experiences, or lack thereof. Much like stepping on a rake, we ask questions after we've already experienced the strike to the forehead like many a cartoon, hoping to understand why it happened. But the question is not about the rake itself; it's about the awareness we bring to our actions. The rakes we step on are not just obstacles, they are markers along the path that point us back to where we lost our attention. So, as we dive into these frequently asked fails, remember: the wisdom is not in avoiding the fail, but in understanding what it reveals about you."*

1) Q: What if I don't have time for all this?

Ah yes, the classic *"I'm too busy"* excuse. Let me guess—you're so busy that you barely have time to blink, let alone work on yourself, right? Well, here's the truth: You *have* time. You're spending it on other things, like scrolling Instagram, watching cat videos, or over-analyzing that one text from three days ago.

Let's get real: Working on yourself doesn't have to take hours. Start small—like *ridiculously* small. Got five minutes? Great. Use it to write one goal, take a deep breath, or do literally anything that moves you closer to progress.

Remember, time isn't something you "find." It's something you *make*. And if Beyoncé can have the same 24 hours a day as the rest of us, you can carve out five minutes to stop stepping on metaphorical rakes.

2) Q: What if I don't feel motivated?

Oh, sweet summer child. If you wait for motivation to magically appear, let me save you some time: It's not coming. Motivation is flaky—it's like that friend who always cancels plans at the last minute. This is why we talk about consistency and doing things you don't want to do because once you start doing them, and doing them consistently, you build your own momentum.

Here's the secret: You don't need motivation to get started. You need *action*. Even the smallest action creates momentum, and once you have momentum, motivation usually follows.

Still not convinced. Fine, try this: Tell yourself you'll work on something for just two minutes. That's it. Two minutes. Most of the time, you'll end up doing more because starting is the hardest part.

And if you don't? Well, congratulations—you just spent two minutes doing something productive instead of Googling "why am I always tired?" again.

3) Q: What if I try and fail?

Oh no, not failure! Anything but that!

Listen, failure is not the monster under your bed. It's not something to be afraid of—it's something to *expect*. In fact, if you're not failing, you're probably not trying hard enough.

Think of failure as your free trial for success. Every time you mess up, you're learning what doesn't work—and that's invaluable. Remember Thomas Edison? He "failed" 1,000 times before inventing the lightbulb. Imagine if he'd given up after attempt #53.

So, go ahead and fail. Fail spectacularly. Just make sure you learn something from it, dust yourself off, and try again. Because the only real failure is giving up entirely.

4) Q: Can I skip the hard parts?

Sure, if you also want to skip the growth, the progress, and the satisfaction of actually achieving something.

Here's the thing: The hard parts are where the magic happens. They're where you learn what you're capable of, build resilience, and prove to yourself that you can handle life's curveballs. Skipping them is like going to the gym and only working out your pinky finger—it might be easy, but it's not going to get you anywhere.

Embrace the hard parts. They're what make the wins feel so damn good.

5) Q: What if I don't know where to start?

Congratulations—you've officially reached Step 1: Admitting you don't know where to start. That's half the battle won right there and knowing is half the battle as G.I. Joe used to say.

Here's the good news: You don't need a perfectly laid-out plan to get started. You just need to take one small, imperfect step. Pick something—anything—and start there.

Still stuck? Let me make it easy for you:

1. Write down one thing you want to change or improve.
2. Break it into the tiniest possible step. (Think: "Google how to start X.")
3. Do that step.

Boom. You've officially started. Now keep going.

6) Q: What if I lose momentum?

First of all, welcome to the club. Losing momentum is part of the process—it happens to *everyone* at some time in their lives. In other words, losing momentum is NORMAL! The key isn't to avoid it entirely; it's to know how to get it back.

Here's your momentum-reboot guide:

1. **Hit the Reset Button**: Give yourself permission to start fresh, no guilt allowed.
2. **Go Back to Basics**: Revisit the small steps that got you moving in the first place. Do those one or two things that got you going to begin with.
3. **Find Your "Why"**: Remind yourself why you started this journey and what you're working toward. Remind yourself that you deserve this success and to learn to be good to yourself. Being good to yourself starts with momentum.
4. **Celebrate Small Wins**: Even tiny victories can reignite your spark. Keep that engine going by celebrating often!

Remember, momentum isn't a straight line. It's a series of starts, stops, and restarts—and that's okay.

7) Q: Why does it feel like everyone else has it all figured out?

Spoiler alert: They don't.

Social media is a highlight reel, not a reality show. No one posts their failures, their meltdowns, or the time they ate an entire pizza while crying about their life choices. You're comparing your behind-the-scenes to someone else's greatest hits—and that's not a fair fight.

The truth is, everyone's figuring it out as they go. So, stop comparing yourself to others and focus on your own journey. You're doing better than you think.

Pause for Reflection:

We all have moments where we trip, stumble, or straight-up face-plant. And while it's tempting to avoid talking about the rakes we've stepped on, the truth is they hold the best lessons. The question isn't "Why did I fail?" but rather "What did I learn?" Think back to a time when you "failed." Did you look at it as a failure, or did you see it as a stepping stone? How did that moment shape who you are today? The rakes are never about the pain—they're about the growth that follows. Now pause and reflect: What rakes have taught you the most? What's one failure you can look at with gratitude instead of regret? In this chapter, we'll dig into the most common "fails" and explore how they hold the key to stepping up stronger the next time.

8) Q: What if I don't believe in myself?

That's okay—I believe in you, and that's a solid starting point.

Self-belief isn't something you're born with; it's something you build. And you build it by proving to yourself, one tiny step at a time, that you're capable.

Here's a trick: Act like the person you want to become. Even if you don't fully believe it yet, pretend you do. Over time, those actions will start to feel more natural, and your confidence will grow.

Fake it till you make it? More like *fake it till you believe it*.

9) Q: How do I deal with people who don't support me?

Ah, the haters. Whether it's a well-meaning family member, a snarky coworker, or your own inner critic, dealing with negativity is tough.

Here's the deal: Not everyone will understand your journey—and that's okay. You're not doing this for them; you're doing it for *you*.

How to Handle the Naysayers:

1. **Set Boundaries**: Politely but firmly shut down negative comments.
2. **Surround Yourself with Support**: Focus on the people who uplift and encourage you.
3. **Prove Them Wrong**: Nothing shuts up a critic faster than success.

And if all else fails, remember: Their opinion doesn't define you—your actions do.

10) Q: What if I'm too tired to work on myself?

First of all, same. We've all been there. The "too tired to adult, too tired to care, too tired to even microwave leftovers" level of exhaustion is real. But here's the thing: You're not too tired to work on yourself—you're just too tired to do it in the way you *think* you should.

When you're running on fumes, the solution isn't to push harder—it's to simplify. Take the pressure off and focus on *tiny* steps that don't feel overwhelming.

Examples for the Exhausted:

- Write down one thing you're grateful for.
- Do one stretch while lying on the floor.
- Drink a glass of water and call it self-care.

Progress doesn't always look like a sprint. Sometimes it looks like a nap followed by one baby step forward.

11) Q: What if I don't want to do the homework?

Oh, you don't want to do the homework? Cool, cool. Let me guess—you're also the kid who pretended their dog ate their science project?

Listen, the homework in this book isn't busywork. It's not here to make your life harder; it's here to make your life *better.* Think of it as a conversation with yourself, a chance to reflect, dream, and take action.

But if the word "homework" makes you break out in hives, let's reframe it. Call it "life experiments" or "fun challenges" or "stuff that might actually help me not hate Mondays." Whatever works. Just do it. You'll thank me later.

12) Q: What if I've already read a million self-help books, and none of them worked?

First of all, kudos for not giving up. Second, let me ask you this: Did you actually *do* anything those books suggested?

Self-help books aren't magic spells. You can't just read them and expect your life to change. You have to *apply* what you learn, even if it feels awkward or uncomfortable at first.

So, instead of asking, *"Will this book work?"* ask yourself, *"Am I willing to work with this book?"* Because if you are, I promise you'll see results—even if they're small at first.

13) Q: Can I skip to the "happy ending" part of life?

Wouldn't that be nice? Just fast-forward through all the hard stuff, land directly in a montage of you living your best life, and call it a day. Unfortunately, life doesn't work like that.

Here's the truth: The "happy ending" isn't a single destination. It's a series of moments you create along the way. It's the joy of small wins, the pride of overcoming challenges, and the peace of knowing you're doing your best.

So, instead of waiting for a happy ending, start creating happy *moments*. Because those moments add up to a life that feels meaningful, fulfilling, and, yes, happy.

14) Q: What if I'm scared of changing?

Of course you're scared. Change is terrifying. It's also exhilarating, necessary, and the only way to grow.

Here's the thing about fear: It's not a stop sign. It's a sign that you're stepping out of your comfort zone—and that's where the magic happens.

Instead of trying to eliminate fear, learn to work with it. Acknowledge it, thank it for trying to protect you, and then move forward anyway. Because the only thing scarier than changing is staying stuck where you are.

15) Q: How do I deal with setbacks that feel like they're never going to end?

Ah, the eternal setback. The thing that makes you want to scream into the void and throw your to-do list out the window. I get it.

Here's the truth: No setback lasts forever, even if it feels like it right now. The key is to focus on what you *can* control and keep moving forward, one tiny step at a time.

Pro Tips for Enduring Long Setbacks:

1. Break your goals into even smaller steps.
2. Celebrate *any* progress, no matter how small.
3. Remind yourself that you've survived tough times before—and you'll survive this, too.

Setbacks don't define you. How you respond to them does.

16) Q: What if I don't like who I am right now?

First, let's get one thing straight: You are not a finished product. You are a work in progress, and that's a beautiful thing.

Not liking who you are right now doesn't mean you're unworthy or unlovable. It just means there's room for growth—and isn't that why you picked up this book in the first place?

Here's a challenge: Instead of focusing on what you don't like about yourself, focus on what you *can* like. Maybe it's your sense of humor, your resilience, or that you're trying to improve. Build on those things, and over time, you'll find more and more reasons to like the person you're becoming.

17) Q: What if I don't know what I want in life?

Welcome to the club. Most people don't know what they want in life, they just pretend they do so they don't have to admit it.

The good news? You don't have to figure it all out right now. Start with what you *don't* want and work backward. Try new things, explore your curiosities, and give yourself permission to change your mind.

Clarity comes from action, not overthinking. So, instead of obsessing over the "right" path, pick a direction and start walking. You'll figure it out as you go.

18) Q: What if I never figure it out?

Spoiler alert: Nobody ever fully figures it out. That's the secret of life, it's not about finding all the answers; it's about learning to ask better questions.

So, instead of worrying about figuring it all out, focus on enjoying the journey. Laugh at the absurdity, celebrate the small wins, and embrace the fact that life is a constant process of learning, growing, and evolving.

Because at the end of the day, the only thing you really need to figure out is this: How to keep showing up, no matter what.

Homework Time:

1. **Reframe a Recent Fail:** Write down a recent failure you've experienced. Now, rewrite the story from a positive angle. What strengths did you discover in yourself through this experience? What did this "failure" teach you that you didn't know before? This exercise helps you see that every fail has the potential to teach you something valuable.

2. **The Next Step Plan:** Think about the next challenge or goal you're pursuing. Write down one potential obstacle or failure that might happen along the way. How will you handle it differently this time? Write down a step-by-step plan to face that failure with resilience and a positive attitude.

3. **Failure Timeline:** Create a timeline of three big "fails" from your life. For each, reflect on the lessons you learned, how you grew, and where that failure led you. This exercise will help you realize that your failures have brought you to where you are today—and that place is far more resilient than you might have realized.

End of Chapter Exercises:

1. **Failure Reflection Journal:** Every day for the next week, journal one small failure or mistake. Don't focus on the negativity. Instead, write about what you learned and how it will help you avoid or handle similar challenges in the future. This is a great way to train your brain to see failure as an opportunity for growth.

2. **Fail-Forward Action Steps:** Choose one current goal or challenge that you're working toward. Write down one way you can "fail forward" on this journey. Perhaps you'll take a risk that might not work out but will teach you something in the process. This exercise helps you practice the art of moving forward in the face of uncertainty.

3. **Create Your "Fail-Friendly" Circle:** Think about the people in your life who support you, even when things don't go as planned. Reach out to them and express your gratitude for their non-judgmental, fail-friendly attitude. Then, set up a time with one of them to talk about a current challenge you're facing. Sometimes, simply sharing our "fails" can turn them into valuable learning experiences.

Key Takeaways:

- **Failure Is Not the End, It's the Beginning:** Failing doesn't mean you're done; it means you've learned something that will help you grow. Every failure is simply a new opportunity to bounce back stronger.

- **Growth Happens Through Adversity:** The tough moments are the ones that teach you the most. Failures show you where you need to grow and what areas of your life require more attention or a change in perspective.

- **Reframing Failure Is Empowering:** Instead of letting failure defeat you, see it as a stepping stone to success. Each failure brings you closer **to achieving your goals because it teaches you what doesn't work.**

- **Don't Fear Failing Forward:** When you fail, fail forward. Take the lesson, adjust, and keep moving. Each failure is a building block for your resilience and success.

- **It's About How You Handle Failure:** The real measure of success isn't how many times you fall; it's how many times you get back up, learn from it, and keep going with more wisdom and experience.

Cheat Sheets & Recaps:

- **Failure = Growth:** Every failure is a lesson in disguise. By embracing failure, you open the door to learning and growth. The more you fail, the stronger you get.

- **Learn from Each Fail:** Every mistake has something valuable to teach. The trick is to listen to the lesson and not dwell on the pain.

- **Failure Is a Stepping Stone:** Don't see failure as an obstacle. See it as a necessary part of your journey. Every failed attempt brings you closer to success.

- **Fail-Forward Mindset:** Embrace the mindset of learning from failure. Don't let setbacks stop you; let them propel you forward with new insights.

- **Resilience Comes from Failing:** Resilience isn't something you're born with; it's something you build through repeated failure and growth. Embrace failure, and it will teach you how to bounce back stronger each time.

Kenism: *"These questions, these 'fails', they are not to be feared. They are signs you are trying, that you are engaging with life's lessons. Just as a tree learns to bend with the wind, you too learn to bend with the challenges. The rakes in your life are not here to punish you, they are here to teach you the art of awareness. Every fail, every stumble, is a step toward greater clarity, deeper understanding. So, when the next fail comes your way, ask yourself not 'why me?' but 'what can I learn? Look for the wisdom you seek; you'll often find it where you least expect.*

Final Thoughts

There you have your most frequently asked fails, lovingly answered with a mix of sarcasm, tough love, and heartfelt advice. If you still have doubts, fears, or excuses, don't worry, they're normal. The important thing is that you're here, you're trying, and you're taking steps toward a better version of you.

And remember: Life isn't about avoiding the rakes—it's about learning to laugh when you step on them and finding the courage to keep moving forward.

Now go out there and show the world what you're made of. You've got this.

TL;DR: Failure is not something to fear—it's a tool for growth. In this chapter, we've learned how to reframe failure as an opportunity to learn and grow. By failing forward and embracing the lessons in every setback, we build resilience and strength. The more we fail, the more we learn. Every failure is a lesson in disguise, and the more we embrace that, the more resilient we become in the face of life's challenges.

Final Things to Think About

So, you've made it to the end of this book! Give yourself a round of applause—or, if you're like me, maybe a quiet nod and a snack. You've just trekked through an entire field of metaphorical rakes and, remarkably, you've come out wiser, stronger, and hopefully, still laughing. That's no small feat, my friend. You've not only faced the chaos of life head-on, but you've also learned how to dance with it. That's progress—and maybe even art.

Before you run off to conquer the world (or, let's be honest, binge-watch something because you've "earned it"), let's pause for a moment to reflect on what you've learned and how you can take these lessons into the next chapter of your life. Spoiler: This is just the beginning.

Why Did You Pick Up This Book?

Be honest—was it because you've been stepping on the same rake over and over, cursing gravity, fate, and possibly your own decision-making skills? And you're afraid to admit your mistakes? Or maybe life just threw a particularly gnarly rake your way, and you're tired of it smacking you in the face. Either way, you're here. You showed up. That alone is a win.

Let's start with a reminder: Life will always have rakes. Some are lying in wait, perfectly positioned to take you out when you're barefoot and distracted. Others are the kind you create yourself by not putting away your emotional, professional, or metaphorical tools. The good news? Every rake is a lesson. The better news? You've learned how to dodge some of them—or at least how to laugh when they hit.

What You've Gained

If this book has done its job (and I really hope it has), you're walking away with a toolkit for life. Here's a quick recap of the lessons, strategies, and awkwardly relatable anecdotes you've encountered along the way:

1. Progress Over Perfection

You've learned that perfection is a myth—an exhausting, unattainable myth that no one really needs in their life. Instead, you've embraced the power of small, imperfect steps. Progress isn't about grand gestures; it's about consistently showing up, even when you don't feel like it.

2. Failures Are Just Feedback

You've reframed failure as a teacher, not a final grade. Every time you've fallen, you've picked yourself up, wiped the metaphorical dirt off your pants, and asked, "What's the lesson here?" Failure doesn't define you; it refines you.

3. Momentum Is Key

Motivation is unreliable—it's like that one flaky friend who swears they'll show up but never does. Momentum, on the other hand, is your dependable sidekick. You've learned to create it, sustain it, and use it to power through the hard days.

4. Resilience Is a Superpower

Life has rakes. Resilience is what keeps you moving, laughing, and learning. You've built your resilience muscle chapter by chapter, proving to yourself that you can handle setbacks with humor and grace.

5. Your Life, Your Rules

You've defined success on your own terms, mapped out your priorities, and embraced a life that feels like yours—not society's, not Instagram's, and definitely not Karen-from-Accounting's.

Your Momentum Maintenance Plan

As you step away from these pages and into your beautifully chaotic life, let's make sure you're equipped to keep the momentum going. After all, this isn't just about surviving the rake-filled garden of life; it's about thriving in it.

1. Keep Moving

Take one small step every day. Whether it's a literal step, like a quick walk, or a figurative one, like sending that email you've been dreading, progress happens one tiny action at a time.

2. Laugh Often

When life hands you lemons—or worse, a rake—laugh. Humor is your greatest ally. Don't be angry with yourself, change your perspective and laugh. Why? Because we all make mistakes, you are normal! Laughing lightens the load, shifts your perspective, and reminds you not to take everything so seriously.

3. Celebrate Small Wins

No win is too small to celebrate. Got out of bed? Win. Finished a project at work? Win. Ate a vegetable? Huge win. Celebrate all!

4. Rest and Reset

Momentum doesn't mean running on empty. Schedule rest like it's a meeting with your most important client—because it is. Without rest, you can't reset, refocus, or keep moving forward.

5. Stay Curious

Keep learning, trying, and experimenting. Life is less about finding answers and more about asking better questions. Curiosity keeps things fresh and prevents you from getting stuck in a rut.

6. Surround Yourself with Good Energy

Your circle matters. Be with people who inspire you, challenge you, and make you laugh. Cut ties with energy vampires—they'll drain your momentum faster than Netflix drains your weekend.

Final Thoughts (With a Side of Snark)

So, what's next? That's entirely up to you. You've got the tools, the mindset, and—most importantly—the resilience to tackle whatever comes your way. Whether your next challenge is a career pivot, or a personal transformation, you're ready.

Remember: Life isn't about avoiding rakes. It's about stepping on them less often, learning when they strike, and finding the humor in the chaos. You're not here to be perfect. You're here to grow, laugh, and keep moving forward, one awkward, glorious step at a time.

Now, go out there and make magic happen—or at least avoid a few more rakes. And if you ever need a reminder of how far you've come, flip back through these pages, laugh at your progress, and keep stepping forward. You've got this.

www.ingramcontent.com/pod-product-compliance
Lightning Source LLC
Chambersburg PA
CBHW060319050426
42449CB00011B/2554